Dedicated To

Hardworking Students at Kota
And
Civil Services Aspirants
And
Their Parents

KOTA CALLING

IS PLAN B READY?

A Chapter In A Day Keep The Depression Away

A Unique Memorable Gift For Teenagers

DEEPAK KHAIRHA IRAS

INDIA • SINGAPORE • MALAYSIA

Copyright © Deepak Khairha 2025
All Rights Reserved.

ISBN
Hardcase 979-8-89673-745-2
Paperback 979-8-89475-970-8

This book has been published with all efforts taken to make the material error-free after the consent of the author. However, the author and the publisher do not assume and hereby disclaim any liability to any party for any loss, damage, or disruption caused by errors or omissions, whether such errors or omissions result from negligence, accident, or any other cause.

While every effort has been made to avoid any mistake or omission, this publication is being sold on the condition and understanding that neither the author nor the publishers or printers would be liable in any manner to any person by reason of any mistake or omission in this publication or for any action taken or omitted to be taken or advice rendered or accepted on the basis of this work. For any defect in printing or binding the publishers will be liable only to replace the defective copy by another copy of this work then available.

Contents

Part I: Tips and Tricks for Scoring High

Part II: Study Efficiently

Acknowledgement

First of all, I want to thank my mother-in-law, Mrs. Sarla Choudha. Her continuous support led to my marriage with her daughter, Richa. Sarla ji is the one person, after God, who is responsible for my marriage, and today, we have a happy family because of her. I will always be indebted to her for ensuring that our marriage happened and was blessed with success.

My father-in-law, Mr. Brijesh Madhav Choudha, has always stood by me as a father figure, especially after my father passed away. His constant support through the challenges in my life has been a true pillar of strength, and for that, I am forever grateful. His guidance is something I will never forget.

I also want to express my heartfelt gratitude to my brother-in-law, Mr. Manish Madhav Choudha, and his wife, Mrs. Pragati Choudha, for their direct and indirect support. Pragati once told me in 2010, "Jijaji, you are blessed by the Goddess of Wisdom, Saraswati Ji, and your mind is your greatest asset." Her words have stayed with me and continue to inspire me.

I want to thank my lovely and beautiful wife, Mrs. Richa Khairha, and our wonderful children—daughter Reet and son Divya. Our children are sweet and humble, possessing countless qualities that inspire me every day—qualities far beyond my own. This year marks the silver jubilee of our marriage, and we have successfully completed 25 years together. Richa, thank you for standing by me through these 25 years, especially for your patience and support when I wake up at 4 a.m. to work on this book. You have been my strength, my balance, and my peace.

This book is a result of not just my efforts but the efforts of many. It was a true team project, and I want to thank all my seniors, friends, and relatives who supported and guided me in writing this book. I would like to thank Mr. D.K. Saraf, Supervisor with Chief PRO, for bringing my ideas to life through brilliant computer graphics. A big thank you as well to Mr. Harshit Shrivastava, Chief PRO West Central Railway, Jabalpur, for his help and contributions.

I want to thank my beloved mother, Late Smt. Kishori Khairha, for her endless love, strength, and guidance. She raised me with courage and kindness, instilling values that shaped my life. Her unwavering support has been my greatest blessing, and her memory continues to inspire me every day.

Last but not least, finally, I want to express my deepest gratitude to my father Late Shri Janki Prasad Khairha, who has been my guiding light and greatest support. His love, wisdom, and sacrifices have shaped who I am today. He taught me the values of kindness, hard work, and perseverance. Every lesson he shared, every moment he spent with me, will remain etched in my heart forever. Though he is no longer with us, his spirit lives on in everything I do. Thank you, Dad, for giving me the strength and foundation to face the world. You will be missed, but never forgotten.

To all of you—thank you, from the bottom of my heart. This book exists because of your support, your belief in me, and your encouragement. I am deeply grateful to each and every one of you.

Once again, thank you all.

Introduction

"Stay away from those people who try to disparage your ambitions. Small minds will always do that, but great minds will give you a feeling that you can become great too."

– Mark Twain

As a reader, I have not seen any good book purely dedicated to students or kids for their inspiration. Most of the books are written for careers after graduation, but this book will be useful for children as young as ten and graduates up to the age of 25. I hope it will benefit them in their careers in general and in their daily lives in particular. All motivational books are meant for persons above 25, but this is an exception.

It is very commonly seen that kids don't listen to their parents. But if the same is said by others or by their teachers, they immediately follow them, and this book will work as a spokesperson for each parent to their kids. I am sure that if kids read this book, then they will follow it because it is a voice of a third person other than their parents.

In this book, I have covered many aspects of life like depression, failure, the role of music and friends in your life, and how to take on challenges. And many minor things that encourage you. These are all real-life examples that modified my life. I have listed all the failures of my life that made me stronger and gave me new strength to go ahead in my life with new energy. I hope this book will encourage students to achieve success in their life and keep them away from depression and suicidal tendencies.

Every project, mission, or target has a reason or a spark behind it. The reason can be anything ranging from fame, money, social service to success in life. Here, also in my case, the purpose of writing this book was to guide the students, those who are appearing in entrance examinations for Engineering, Medical, etc. Every year, the student who tries to commit suicide can be guided timely to avoid such cases and will be motivated to perform well in the examination. Another purpose of the book is to guide the graduates who are appearing in the Civil Services or State Services or any other examination so that they can improve scores in their respective examinations.

Here I have divided the audience of the book into four categories. First, there are the students who are in the standard 9th to 12th; second, those who are appearing in Engineering, Medical, or Law entrance examinations; third, those who are appearing in the Civil Services, State Service Examination, etc., for getting jobs; and the last, the fourth one, is the parents who are sending their kids for these examinations in coaching classes away from their homes.

When I was posted in Kota as a Financial Adviser in the railway in 2021, every alternate week I used to read headlines in newspapers about the suicides committed by students studying for Engineering or Medical entrance examinations. Kota is the hub of coaching classes for Engineering and Medical entrance exams. There are nearly 3 lakh students who come to this city every year to attend coaching for Engineering and Medical. Every year, nearly 20 to 25 students commit suicide due to depression caused by exam failures.

Last year, the Rajasthan government set up a committee to study such cases and plan strategies to prevent them. However, the government alone cannot take effective action; they can only issue guidelines to hostel management. These guidelines may include fitting safety devices in fans, locking the terrace to prevent students from accessing the roof, installing nets near the first floor, and covering balconies to deter students from attempting to jump. Coaching classes need to involve counsellors and psychologists to address these issues.

These are all the localised preventions by the hostel or the coaching management, but there are many means outside these campuses of hostels and coaching centres to take such dire steps by the students. We cannot keep a watch on each and every student living here. Here, a better strategy would be, instead of targeting the physical part, to target the mental part of students and parents both simultaneously.

The primary role of parents here is to know, understand, and support the talent and the capability of their kids, so they can guide their kids to choose the line best suited for them. Setting abnormally high targets by kids is also sometimes detrimental to their lives. Here parents have to encourage their kids instead of discouraging them, especially if they are setting very high targets compared to their talent. Rather, parents have to tell them to go step by step and achieve smaller targets, then aspire for the bigger ones. Directly setting very high targets may lead to depression in case of failure.

Here in this book, I covered the Dos and Don'ts for all four categories of audience. What they are doing wrong and what they ought to do are discussed in great detail. Suicide is linked to prolonged depression, which in turn is linked to failure or a poor score in a test or exam, which is finally related to poor strategy or planning for the various exams.

Therefore, rather than controlling the suicide cases, it is better to target the exam strategy and planning part. This way, hardly anyone will fail, and no one will go into depression. Eventually, suicide cases will vanish from Kota and other places. Here, we have to keep in mind that there are only limited seats in the examinations. Not everyone can get selected, but there are many avenues for your career. Life is much bigger than a career, job, or future. **A FAILURE IN ONE EXAM CANNOT DETERMINE YOUR ENTIRE FUTURE.**

A. What Is Here For 9th To 12th-class Students?

The period between classes from 9th to 12th is very crucial for all the students because it shapes the future and career of the students. Generally, it is seen that the students, those who were performing well before 9th, go down in performance after 9th. The same consistency is required for 9th to 12th classes, and after that also for a successful career.

The First Target group for this book is the students in 9th to 12th standard because at this age, the students are in a very tender stage and they can change their reading habits by taking best suggested tricks from this book and adopt in their lives, whatever suits them. The book can also be helpful for the students below 9th standard if their parents can read it and explain the tricks and tips given in this book. The students from standard 5th to 8th are hardly interested to read such novel type of books because they already have a big curriculum to complete every year. Hence, I request, all the parents whose kids are in class 5th to 8th, to kindly go through the book and guide your wards for better performance in their classes.

There are many tips, tricks, or strategies in this book. These can become the foundation stones for your wards in shaping their future. If the parents want their wards to become an IAS, IPS, doctor, engineer, or a reputed lawyer, then it will be very helpful for such kids. After reading this book, they will be filled with full energy and vigour to crack any exams.

This book covers what losers generally miss out on and what winners generally do for their success. There is hardly a thin line gap between the strategies of winners and losers; both do the hard work almost equally, but the **winners do it more strategically and systematically** in a planned way.

I would request all parents to give this book to your wards if they are mature enough to read it themselves. If they are not able to understand it, then parents should first read it and tell their wards about the study plan given in this book. Let them choose whatever suits them for adopting in their day-to-day lives for better performance in their studies. If your kids are in 9th to 12th standard, then it is better if they directly read this book without your intervention, but you have to gift it to them. It will be the best gift in their lives because it will shape their future.

B. For Those Aspiring For Medical Or Engineering Entrance Exams

The next target audience for this book is the students above 12th standard or even in 12th standard, those who are aspiring for Medical, Engineering, or Law entrance examinations. They are slightly more mature compared to the previous category; hence, this book will be more helpful for them as it is written with this group of students in mind.

Such are the groups living a thousand kilometres away from their home for preparation of Medical or Engineering entrance examinations. The main study centre for these students is Kota, where lakhs of students are studying and competing for various Medical and Engineering Tests.

The very purpose of this book is to encourage students of this group to excel in exams and to keep them away from depression and suicidal tendencies. The book is based on the TTS plan, which means Tips, Tricks, and Strategies for solving papers and scoring better in examinations. I am sure that by adopting these strategies, the scores will improve in class tests as well as in the main entrance examination.

The book covers nearly 45 chapters dedicated to the planning and strategy for examination so that study will not be a burden, rather it becomes a means of entertainment for you or works like a hobby for you. The books and the syllabus are the same for all students, but some are studying it with interest, and others feel it like a burden. Reading this book will spark an ignition in your mind to study hard to realise your ambitions and dreams. This book will work as a catalyst for your career.

Every talent is inside you only. The only role of this book will be to help you plan your study in a systematic way so as to have maximum outcomes. The book covers the main chapters on how to answer, whether it is Multiple Choice Questions (MCQ) papers or the Subjective Style papers, how to plan your study so that you will not forget the things you read, the optimum utilisation of the time to extract the maximum benefit in a day, how to study so that the chapter will be interesting, how to plan a day earlier so that you will wake up with full energy in the morning, whether you have to read by multiple books or by only one book, 70:20:10

strategy for preparation of various exams, how to handle your mistakes and failures in your life so that you will not go into deep depression, how to handle the fear and pressure of exams, how to recharge yourself if you are drained out of energy for the next slot of study session, how to choose the topics or the subjects for the morning so that you will not feel sleepy, how to make the notes for the exam so that even in an hour you can revise your whole syllabus. Such types of issues are discussed in detail in this book for the maximum benefits of the students.

Since the book is written based on this group as a target, it is also mentioned here what such students should do to avoid the pressure of the study into their minds. Finally, they can avoid the depression that can creep into their minds. I am sure that after reading this book, the depression will vanish from the lives of the students, giving them a fresh lease of life.

C. A Treatise for Civil Services

The Civil Services aspirants are the third targeted audience for this book. Every year, around three lakh graduates or postgraduate students appear in the Civil Services examination, and nearly 10 lakh students appear in the State Services examination. However, only 600 to 700 candidates get selected in the Civil Services. Additionally, around 3000 candidates get selected in State Services every year, meaning less than 0.3% of students are selected in these exams.

There is a lot of difference in Civil Services exams and the other exams for jobs. In other exams, you can decide overnight, appear, and you may qualify, but in Civil Services, it is not an overnight decision; rather, it is a decision taken by students when they are in standard 8th or 9th. The journey of preparation starts at a very tender age for students. There are very exceptional students who decide quite late in their student life and then manage to get through, but such cases are very rare.

Similarly, my journey also started from my standard 8th for Civil Service examination. There was no one in my home town Panna (Madhya Pradesh) to guide me for this exam. I used to sit in my shop at Panna to assist my father during the period from 1985 to 1990. I was motivated by seeing the red-light vehicles of the Collector and SP passing through my shop at 10:00 a.m. in the morning and then again in the evening at nearly 7:00 p.m. After that, there was a caravan of vehicles for Deputy Collector, DSP, Tehsildar, Inspector, etc.

Whenever any Sub Engineer of PWD, PHED, or Irrigation department came to my shop, my father personally offered him water and tea. My father always used to say "Sir" or "Sahab" in respect of his government job. Papa was giving so much respect to him because he wanted to get the business and order from that engineer for supply to government department. But giving so much respect to him was hurting me. After their tea, my papa used to give me a two rupee note to go to the paan shop (betel leaves shop) to offer him the paan and supari. After finishing all these, the Sub Engineer used to commit to the next order from my shop.

It was not a win-win situation for us; rather, it was a win-win-win situation for us. One win for my father, another win for the government supervisor, and the last, third win was for me. By watching this 30-minute reality show, I was inspired to study hard daily. Hence, I used to study every day until 12:00 at night and would get up at 4:00 a.m. because I was scared about my future. I did not want to end up serving water, tea, or paan supari to a government engineer. These two things, first, the caravan of vehicles of the collector, and second, the respect shown by my father to the government officer, were the motivational forces behind my preparation for Civil Services.I did not want to go back to that monotonous life of a shopkeeper.

At that time, no good book was available in any shop at Panna for self-help or guidance. The only books available were the textbooks of the syllabus and a few magazines or comics at the bus stand booksellers' shop. Hence, the purpose of writing this book is to guide the students who are staying in the villages and have never seen the life of cities. Today, everything is available on the net to buy and that too delivered in a few days to your home.

This book also covers the strategy for the preparation of Civil Services. It guides you on how to solve multiple-choice questions in prelims without compromising on speed or accuracy. It also advises on how to draft answers for subjective questions and plan essay writing within a 2-3 hour timeframe for the Civil Service examination. The Civil Service examination requires a minimum of 12 hours of study daily. The book will guide you on how to increase your study stamina from 6 hours to 12 hours through small planning and tricks so that you do not feel bored with studying. It explains how to schedule your daily study routine and make the best use of the 24 hours available so that you do not feel enervated or exhausted. It also covers how to choose topics or subjects for morning or late-night study sessions to avoid feeling sleepy.

Additionally, it provides guidance on studying in a way that enhances recall and retention of information over time. The book explains how to create self-made notes and the format of these notes to facilitate quick preparation during exam days. It also offers tips on how to efficiently revise your entire syllabus depending on the time available for exam preparation.

You can see from the results of the Civil Service every year that only average students, those who are hardworking, although may not be exceptionally intelligent, get selected. Only a few candidates, those who are the wards of Civil Servants, get selected. You can see that most of the sons or daughters of the Civil Servants are not getting selected in this exam. Either they don't want to join the Civil Services or they could not get through this exam, even though they have everything needed for it: money, guidance, time, and financial security. Hence, it is all your internal ambitions, your own desires, or dreams to become IAS, IPS. No one can force you to appear in these exams. The only thing your parents can do is to motivate you or they can help you financially. A slight motivation you can also get from this book after reading it.

I am sure the money cannot be a hurdle if you are preparing for the Civil Services exam because the total expenditure for this exam is only nominal. The only expenses are for your books, newspapers, or if you are staying in metro cities like Delhi, Allahabad, or Patna, then day-to-day expenditures are the only costs you have to bear. Otherwise, hardly any expenditure is required for such exams, making it the cheapest exam in terms of money.

All the best for your journey to the Civil Services.

D. Parents, Be Polite, Handle Your Wards Carefully.

It is a very common thing among most of the Indian parents that once they spend money on the education of their wards, especially during the entrance examination of Medical or Engineering, or during the exam for the job (like Civil Services, etc.), they expect a Rate of Return on that investment in the form of selection in Medical or Engineering, or in the form of a good government job. This mentality of most of the Indian parents has to be changed so that they will not think about returns on these expenses, and they should not treat it as an investment. It is just like any other expenditure they do for purchasing a four-wheeler, bike, or any other household items like a fridge, TV, etc. Do we really think that what a four-wheeler, TV, or anything else gives us anything in return? It is just comfort or happiness we get from these things.

All parents have to think in a similar fashion for all the expenses incurred on the education of kids. Don't expect immediate returns or results for these expenditures. These are all human resource investments, unlike other investments; it may take time to give you results. If you are lucky, then you will get immediate results, but if you are not that lucky, then you will get results later. But your money will not go to waste; it will come back either immediately or as a value addition in the talent or calibre of your wards.

Hence, after reading this book, the parents should understand that all these expenses on their wards are normal expenses, so they should not wait daily for a return on this. If your wards are appearing in the entrance exam of Medical or Engineering, then be very careful when handling them. Be polite and gentle in your approach. Never discuss in front of them the money you are spending on their education. They are at a very tender age and are emotional and touchy about such matters. They may start thinking that in case of failure in the exam, all their parents' money will be wasted.

If your son or daughter is an average student, never compare him or her with another outstanding sibling or with any other person in your neighbourhood or among your relatives. Parents have to assure their children that in case of failure, there is a **plan B** ready for them. This plan could be a business or another college or job opportunity. You need to reassure them that **life is much bigger than college, job, career, and future**. After hearing such statements from parents, children will feel secure in life and believe that there will be someone supporting them in case of failure. Parents should appreciate their children's every achievement and console them in case of any setbacks. Stay in touch with them all the time so that they never feel lonely.

Whenever your wards are appearing in entrance exams, whether staying with you or living away from home, always communicate with them. They will feel happy, and your 5 minutes of talk will encourage them to study and make them feel protected. Never send your wards forcefully for the preparation of entrance examinations if they are not willing to prepare. Instead, the request should come from them that they want to go for the exam preparation. Even after sending them for these preparations, stay in touch with their colleagues so that you can keep track of the progress of your wards, their studies, their class rank, or any setbacks in their lives. If you notice any behavioural changes in your wards, whether directly or indirectly through their colleagues, consider it an alarm. Take immediate corrective action. **Remember, life is more precious than anything else.**

Here, parents have to strike a balance. On the one hand, they have to keep a watch on their kids for their scores and ranks and console them politely if needed. On the other hand, they have to be in touch with them, encourage them, and reassure them that there is a plan B ready as an alternative. Always visit the kids quarterly according to their comfort, if they are living away from home, so that their studies will not be affected.

If your son or daughter is very emotional and touchy, and if as parents, you fail on any of the above points, then they will go into depression. Therefore, in this book, I have covered what parents need to do so that their children will perform better in exams and avoid themselves from going into depression. By adopting these strategies, we can ultimately reduce the number of suicide cases in Kota or elsewhere.

Secondly, if your son or daughter is preparing for Civil Services examinations to secure a government job, they are likely mature enough at this stage. Therefore, you do not need to communicate with them daily; instead, you can call them weekly. However, during this period, the bombarding may come from relatives or neighbours. They may make comments such as, "What happened? This year again, he or she could not get selected." "Age is increasing, no one will marry her after that age," if she is a girl, etc. Just ignore such comments from others.

The Civil Service takes a full year for the exam, and a minimum of 1 year is needed for preparation. If you are selected on the first attempt, then also a minimum of 2 years have passed. However, selection on the first attempt is very difficult. Even if you achieve the rank but not the service of your choice, you will have to reappear. Therefore, Civil Service is a project of 3 to 4 years, so it is advised not to expect premature results in a year.

Even if your ward gets selected or not selected in a year, then also don't force him or her to get married. Instead, allow him or her to appear again for rank improvement or to try to get selected next year with full energy. After getting selected in the Civil Service examination, they will have hundreds of marriage proposals.

In both the above cases, parents have to have **patience, patience, and patience.**

My Apology

Here I want to extend my apology to the readers of this book on various points because they may differ on various aspects of the book given for the guidance of students. I have given most general patterns of the society or the trends in the society. There may be some deviations or differences of opinion on any point. So, instead of doing an argument over that, I want to give my apology if anyone hurts from my analogy or from given real-life examples. The apology covers various points as given below:

To start with, my first apology is on the language of the book. Since I am from a Hindi medium background, the English used is straightforward so that everyone can understand. There may not be smoothness, rhythm, or a good flow in the content, but the purpose is to convey my ideas to all students, Civil Services aspirants, and ultimately to the parents of these two. Hence, just focus on the ideas and overlook the language for the time being.

The chapters are distributed randomly. In other books, specifically novels, there is a flow or order and a timeline of events, but in this book, since there are chapters with ideas, tips, tricks, or strategies, the sequence of chapters hardly matters. Some chapters you may not find in order, so just ignore this aspect. You can read the book from any page. My purpose is just to give you the best of me and from my experiences.

I have used an empirical formula for the "Success," just to explain to you the correlation of success with hard work, IQ (Intelligence Quotient), and luck factor. I am using the term 'Variable Constant' for 'c' because it remains constant for a certain period of time, but eventually changes its value. I have no technical basis to prove the formula, but it is solely for illustrative purposes so that you can understand the value of hard work, luck, and intelligence.

In the 70:20:10 strategy, I have taken these three values randomly based on the trends in various exams. These are approximate average values; there may be minor variation in the values of each item. It can be 65:30:5 or 60:30:10, etc., but my purpose is to explain the toughness of questions in exams.

I have given all the real-life examples just to explain the experiences of my life. It may or may not suit you, but you can adopt the best suited for you and ignore the ones you don't like, or you can modify them to have the best one from my various strategies and tips.

I have given simple food habits during the exam or for the whole year. You can take the items best suited for you because taking food is very specific to community, culture, and geographical area. I gave the best food habits for students in general; you can modify as per the bodily need and availability of food in your family and area.

I have gleaned various lessons from my colleagues, seniors, and teachers. You may not find an exact analogy or guidance, but you can use my life as an example to learn from others if someone guides you.

There are many common tips which you may find in other chapters because some chapters are correlated with each other. You may notice a repetition of certain points, but the purpose of this repetitiveness is to emphasise those points.

I am using the word girlfriend, boyfriend, smoking, or drinks just to guide you. Please don't take these words otherwise. The purpose is simply to keep you away from these during your study life.

I have used the word depression and suicide in this book. Suicide is a very extreme word. I should not have used this word in this book for the guidance of students. But this suicide only inspired me to write the book so that such suicidal cases can be stopped from India in general, and from Kota in particular.

I have used the words "pampered kids" and "emotional kids" for today's generation. Here, the purpose is not to hurt the young generation, but I want to tell the readers of this book that there are some pampered kids. However, in general, not all rich kids are pampered.

I have used the word "waste" for the initial phase so that parents will not calculate the daily returns on that. I treat this expense on the education of kids as any other expenses of the family. Hence, don't wait for its return. The return will come one day in any form, either as a final selection or as a value addition in the personality of the student. One day, this waste will become the best investment, if you just forget the accounting of its returns.

I have used the line that "it is difficult to maintain the rank for all-time toppers because they have no one to compete or follow."

It does not mean that they cannot maintain the rank. I am not challenging or hurting the feelings of all-time toppers; they can also be the final topper in life.

I supported the old system of PET and PMT conducted by states. It is my personal opinion because at that time there were hardly any cases of suicide in the 1980s or 90s. The system was a good example of decentralisation of power to states, but due to some corruption cases in PET and PMT, the Central Government has started a centralised system of entrance for Engineering and Medical.

I have appreciated the way of writing of Shri Khushwant Singh Ji. He has written some books for adults only, so please don't take it otherwise. I appreciated his command and flow in English. It is my personal opinion about his novels. I am not recommending any adult book for the students written by Shri Khushwant Singh Ji.

Here in this book, I suggested burning agarbatti or incense sticks. The purpose is not religious here or to hurt any religious group. Rather, it is suggested to increase your stamina for single study in one stretch. The burning of incense sticks may not suit many students, specifically asthmatic patients; hence, I recommend burning it only if it suits you and keeping it in an open space rather than in a closed room.

I have given two speed graphs generally followed by students during examinations for solving the papers. There is no scientific base for it; rather, it is an illustration so that you can understand the value of accuracy in replying to the question with speed.

I have used the term "final failure" to compare it with "immediate failure," but there is no such term as "final failure" for hardworking people. Hardworking students can experience immediate failure in their lives, but eventually, they succeed in one field or another; they never fail finally.

I have used the word loser; rather the more appropriate word is unsuccessful candidates. In case if you cannot qualify any exam or competition, then don't consider yourself as a loser; instead, it is your immediate failure. Here, losers are those who don't compete, don't participate, or don't do hard work. Hence, hardworking students can never be losers; they can be unsuccessful for any specific exam, but in their lives, they will always be the winners, not the losers.

In many places, I have used the word HE only. He stands for both, whether girl or boy. So please don't take it otherwise. I am not prejudiced against any gender. In almost all legal books or codes, the word HE includes SHE also.

Why Suicide?: A Chapter in a Day Keep the Depression Away

Every year in Kota, many students commit suicide. Last year in 2023, nearly 25 students committed suicide. I was motivated to write this book to stop such cases of suicides and to save the precious lives of the students who are at a very tender age. The word 'suicide' is made up of two sub-words: 'Sui,' meaning 'self,' and 'cide,' meaning 'to kill.' Therefore, suicide means 'to kill oneself. Life is the biggest gift given by God through your parents; we should not end it so easily. You have no right to spoil the gift given by God. Here, the issue is **Why Suicide**. Generally, it is seen that many teenagers commit suicide every year due to love, study, or failure. The recent trend is seen in study and failure in examinations.

The depression is the precondition of suicide. Here, the parents or the students can control it and can avoid such cases of depression. The depressions come into the minds of the emotional students who are very sensitive to the reactions of others in case of failure.

Whenever you feel depressed, you have to first recognise it. The major symptoms of depression are long thinking about your future anxiously, feeling insecure about your education, starting to avoid the group, experiencing sleeplessness or insomnia, loving to be in isolation and alone. You will start thinking that you are a loser in life. Whenever such thoughts come into your mind, immediately tell your parents, friends, and tutors, and consult a psychologist.

Whenever such depression comes to your mind, try to find out the root cause of the depression and try to avoid it. Think about the steps given below to lead a normal life and avoid indulging in suicidal tendencies.

First, if the cause of depression is poor results in examinations or a low score on a test paper, then try to adjust your targets and goals according to your abilities. It is not feasible for every candidate to secure a place in the computer branch at IIT Mumbai, become an IAS officer in the Civil Service, study at AIIMS Delhi for Medical, or attend Bangalore NLU for law studies. Besides the top branches or colleges, there are many other good colleges or job opportunities available. Failing to secure a place in the best college, branch, or job does not signify the end of life. Life offers much more than the future in specific field. Therefore, set your goals according to your capabilities; other colleges are equally good compared to the best ones.

Secondly, suicide is the extreme and worst form of depression. It is, in fact, the end and a pathetic result of depression. If you could control things at the level of depression, that means you have full control over all your senses and over your mind. Don't set impossible targets that are beyond your capacity or capability. Always share your problems with your parents; they are your best friends when it comes to resolving issues and will guide you in the best way. Depression is the cause of suicide and also is the initial stage of suicidal tendencies. At all costs, you have to avoid depression.

It is very difficult to understand the meaning and physical or mental sense of depression. You may feel like not doing anything and having too much fear of the future as well as of present. It generates a lethargic lifestyle with sleeping habits, leading to avoiding the company of others and having too much anxiety about your own life, as well as the lives of your family members.

Suicide is very easy to do, but **Life Is A Great Gift From God. So, Why Kill Yourself**? Career is nothing compared to life; therefore, never think of suicide. Always think a hundred times about your family and parents before committing this act. Soon, you will see that such thoughts will vanish from your mind.

Part I

TIPS AND TRICKS FOR SCORING HIGH

01

Multiple Books Versus Best Book

"Success is not final; failure is not fatal. It is the courage to continue that counts."

– Winston S. Churchill

During my Bilaspur posting, just before my tenure of Kota, one day I counted the total pages of my daughter's books for the Engineering Entrance test for standard 11th and 12th. The total number of pages came out to be nearly 36,000 for two years, covering all textbooks, reference books, and books with numerical and multiple-choice questions (MCQs). These are the total pages in all books she has to read in both classes, mainly textbooks, reference books, and books containing numerical and MCQs. Based on that, she has to read an average of fifty new pages each day. It is an impossible task to cover because she not only has to read these new fifty pages daily but also to revise the previous day's pages for tests in between.

The counting is given assuming that you don't fall sick and have not wasted a single day. During these two years, you have to go for final exams and other tests conducted by coaching classes or the school. Hence, it is better to study by reading only one best book and keep other books as reference books.

If you don't know which is the best book among many, then consult your teachers or seniors; they can tell you the best book for physics, chemistry, maths, biology, or any arts subject. Even if they are not able to tell the best one, you can read multiple books once and choose the best one for regular study and to appear in tests or examinations.

It is generally seen that students keep multiple books (say, five books) for any subject, such as physics, and they read one chapter from these five books. However, at the time of examination, they leave many chapters. Hence, it is better to complete all chapters from one book. If you find difficulty in understanding any topic or in solving any problem, then only read another reference book. There are multiple benefits of reading only one book that is best, instead of reading many books on that subject.

Firstly, you will be able to complete the syllabus on time, and you will have sufficient time for revising the book.

Secondly, by reading the same book repeatedly, it will be easier to memorise. After solving the same problems repeatedly, you will find it easier to solve them, and both your speed and accuracy will improve.

Our mind captures the snaps of the pages in our memory. It remembers as per the placement of the diagram on any part of the page, like left, right, upper, or lower part of the pages. You always remember that this item is printed in which part of two opened pages of any chapter. Hence, reading many times that unique book will imprint in your brain the sequence of the chapters, but if you read multiple books, then the same diagram or the definition is printed in various parts of the pages; hence, it is very difficult to have a memory print in your mind.

Our memory is also linked with colours; hence, whenever you read any chapter, use highlighters to highlight the relevant lines, figures, dates, values, or formulae with various colours. It will enhance your memory, and you need not search for that figure or line by reading the whole page. A coloured picture of the highlighted page will imprint in your brain's memory.

In India, for Civil Services and State Public Services examinations, as well as for JEE, NEET, and AIIMS, the books published by NCERT are best designed to provide students with complete knowledge and a strong foundation of concepts. Hence, before reading any other book, I request students to kindly read these books first and only then consider other options. These basic books offer full clarity to the students; everything is precisely written with great attention to minute details by the best teachers and professors of India.

Another strategy is that you can make self-handwritten notes from the best book if you have sufficient time. Although it is a time-consuming and a little bit boring process, it will make it easier to revise during your examinations. In few hours, you can easily remember the whole content of your notes. After multiple revisions, you just need to flip the pages, and you will recall everything to write in the examination. Hence, your 500-page book will condense to 150 pages of your notes. You can also write some problems or numericals from reference books that are not available in your best book, making it handy to carry one copy instead of carrying multiple books.

After reading this copy multiple times, you can make a summary of this copy in 5 to 6 pages, including important figures, dates, diagrams, data, or formulae. It will be useful for recalling the whole copy just a day before the examination, for example in physics and maths, make 5 to 6 of these pages with formulae and values of various constants, etc., for biology, draw important diagrams, and for arts or humanities subjects, the dates of historical events, names of persons, etc., can be mentioned. These pages can be used for revision a day before the exam or if you have left a few hours for examination. Then comes the micro notes of A4 size pages, which you can get laminated as well. These A4 size notes you can read just before the examination, like various Sections of IPC, Cr.PC, Articles of the Constitution for the law students, or values or formulae for the maths or physics students, or diagrams or tough names of species and genus for the bio students.

Hence, I suggested three types of self-notes. First is the big copy of 150 to 200 pages. You can read it whenever you have sufficient time. Kindly read it again and again to remember. The whole year, you have to read this only. Second is 5 to 6 pages summarised notes, based on your copy. You can read it during the gap of your examination or just a day before your examination. And the last one is the one-page laminate of A4 size paper to read just before the examination or during the interval between two examinations or tests.

02

How to Score Better

"The only one who can tell you, "You can't win," is you, and you don't have to listen."

– Jessica Ennis

If we compare the performance of two similar aptitude guys having similar circumstances or resources, then you will find that there is a wide gap in their scores; one is extremely good, and the other one performed average. Here, the difference lies in the strategy of each one and their reading styles and habits.

So, I am giving some suggestions which are also there in other chapters of this book, and I am repeating them again for better clarity for the readers of this book. If you are a student of physics and mathematics, then solve the derivation or proof of various formulae repeatedly. Prove the theorem-type questions over and over in mathematics. By repetitively solving the derivations, you will be able to solve the questions faster, and it will also clear the concept or doubt of that topic. A higher speed in solving such questions will give you spare time in exams so that you can use that time for new or tough questions.

Always use A4 paper for writing formulae and values of various constants and stick those on the wall in front of your table, so that you will not waste time searching for these formulae. By looking at them 15 times daily, you will recall them easily whenever you require them in an exam. Revision is very necessary for the exam; hence, whatever you study a day before, try to revise those things for at least one hour. This serves two purposes: first, it will clear your concepts and doubts, and second, you will remember it forever. For biology, law, and humanities subjects, you can use A4 paper in front of your table for writing names, diagrams, dates, sections, and articles for ready reference. Therefore, practice, practice, and practice for derivation in physics and theorem in mathematics, and revise, revise, and revise for biology, law, and humanities papers. In physics or mathematics, you have to remember formulae repeatedly. In some questions that have traps or tricks, mark them differently as important tricky questions so that when there is a trap, you will double your attention to remember that.

Always make tips or keywords to remember the whole paragraph so that by those tips, you will remember or recall that paragraph. You can then narrate it in the exam easily using that keyword and write the whole story or derivation. Make an A4 size sheet just to read in 15 minutes to revise everything on the day of the examination. This A4 sheet should contain your formulae, diagrams, dates, or anything you want to revise just before your examination.

Always attempt the first question very patiently. In theoretical papers, start with good handwriting, and for multiple-choice questions (MCQ), at least five questions should be given more time to get speed and confidence for later questions. Revise, revise, and revise for getting good speed in solving questions and for better understanding of the next chapter. For commamding good speed of study in any class, it is beneficial to revise previous classes' books of the field of your interest so that your speed of understanding will be very fast in the current class.

03

Compete with Yourself

"Alone, we can do so little; together, we can do so much."

– Helen Keller

There are three types of students who are affected by the achievements of other students. First, those who are encouraged by the achievements of their colleagues and seniors; second, those who feel either jealous or discouraged by the achievements of successful candidates; and the third, those who are hardly affected or unfazed either way. The best among the three are the students who are encouraged by the success of others. They always try to follow successful candidates and strive further in their lives to achieve such success. If you fall into the second category and feel discouraged or jealous by the success of others, then first try to change your nature.

Take the success of colleagues positively and try to improve yourself. Even if you are not able to change yourself, then adopt the following strategy.

If you are very emotional and feel depressed by hearing the achievements of other students, then just ignore such news and start comparing and competing with yourself. Here, you have to give your 100% and try to do better the next day compared to the previous day's performance. Make your own targets and break them regularly. You will never feel jealous or depressed when competing against yourself.

I will tell you later in another chapter of the book to make a diary for noting down the longest single sitting duration and the longest total study hours in a day. Whenever you break such a record, note down the date and mark it with a star. To enhance the single sitting time, you can use a big incense stick (agarbatti) with a burning time of 2 to 3 hours. Do not stop studying or leave the chair until it burns completely. If you have any other engagements and cannot study on a particular day, make up for the lost time the next day. For achievers, they themselves are their biggest competitors. They always strive to perform better than their previous achievements and aim for further improvement.

Generally, it is seen that parents compare their kids with other successful candidates and expect the same achievements from their kids, even though the kids may not have such calibre. Hence, it is always recommended for parents not to make such comments in front of their kids if they are very emotional and touchy. At the same time, I also request the student to ignore such comments from their parents. Just focus on your mission and ignore such stray things; you must be unfazed by such comparisons. It is the best remedy to avoid depression during your study life.

04

Mehnat x Intelligence (100 x 100 = 10000)

"Talent wins games, but teamwork and intelligence win championships."

– Michael Jordan

Your success is a function of two things. First, there is Mehnat (labour or hard work), and second, there is your Intelligence (wisdom or IQ). The second one, Intelligence, is God-gifted; hardly can you change it, but the hard work or labour is in your hands. I am providing a mathematical illustration just for your understanding. These are merely empirical formulae, not based on exact values or calculations.

S (Success) = f {L (labour) and I (intelligence)}

$S = c*(L*I)$

You can say that Success is a function of your labour and your intelligence, since each one of these components directly increases your chances of success. Hence, you can say that success is directly proportional to the labour and intelligence.

Here, 'c' is a variable constant that changes with time; it is a favourable luck factor. The value of 'c' can range from 0 to 1, depending on your stars. Hence, we give equal weightage to labour and intelligence, assuming 100 for each, and 'c' has values ranging from 0 to 1. Here, I am referring to 'c' as a variable constant in contrast with the other constants, which are universally fixed, because 'c' has a fixed value for a particular time and changes with time according to your luck and stars.

$$S = c*(L*I)$$

$$S_{Max} = 1 * (100 * 100) = 10,000 \text{ (Maximum Value of S)}$$

$$S_{Min} = 0 \text{ (Minimum Value of S)}$$

Then, S (Success) lies in the range of 0 to 10,000.

$$S = c* (L*I)$$

Just have a look at each multiplier. 'c' has the capacity of reducing success to zero, and 'c' is the most powerful factor among these because if you are born with a value of 100 for Intelligence and you are putting in 100 units of labour, then also it is quite possible that you will not achieve success. If the value of 'c' during any exam is zero, then your net result becomes zero and you may not succeed in that exam.

$$S = 0*(100*100) = 0$$

Few examples when 'c' becomes zero: when you lose the flight for your final interview, or you wrongly mark the answer in a multiple-choice question paper by a single shifting, or you fall sick during the most sensitive paper, or you meet with an accident. Sometimes a small mistake in life or a small thing in your life can reduce the value of 'c' to 0, but remember the value of 'c' is not always zero. It is a variable constant depending on your luck and stars. If today it is zero, then next time it may become one, so don't lose hope and keep 'L' and 'I' as high as possible.

$c = f(t)$

$c_{max} = 1$, (Luck is fully favourable)

$c_{min} = 0$, (Highly adverse time)

Here 't' represents time. 't' can change the value of 'c' based on your luck. So, you might have seen that with the same labour and intelligence, a person fails badly in the first year, and in the next year, he or she tops in the whole country.

Mind one thing here 'L', you can change from 0 to 100, but "I", you cannot change too much because it is a God's gift, but you can change 'I' also, but derivatively, that too indirectly by learning new things and keep on reading or by increasing reading habits. It is again indirectly dependent upon the 'L' (hard work); hence, to some extent, you can change 'I' fractionally, that too indirectly, through more input in 'L'.

The formula is most beautifully understood by the students of Bihar. In every exam whether NEET, JEE or IAS (Medical entrance examination, Engineering entrance examination or Civil Service examination respectively), the ratios of these guys are always highest among successful candidates because the high 'I' value guys from Bihar got selected because they are very intelligent students in whole life of their career, at the same time the below average student of Bihar also got selected in the exam because his lower intelligence value of 'I', he covers up by extra value of 'L' that is by making extra labour.

Bihar's intelligent guy (if luck is favourable, c=1)

$S = 1 * (50 * 80) = 4000$

Bihar's average guy, or below-average guy (if luck is favourable, c=1).

$S = 1 * (100 * 40) = 4000$

We can see that an intelligent guy from Bihar has a score of 4000 even if he only does a few hours of labour (50% effort only). However, an average or below-average student from Bihar can also achieve a good score of 4000 for success by just having 'L' as 100, even though they have a score of forty in intelligence.

The students from Bihar are very hardworking, and their mission, focus, or target is very clear. They keep doing hard work and they never are scared of such labour and pain, and finally, one day they get selected. They know the concept of life that a few years of hard work can give you lifelong happiness.

Here you can see that the average value of 'L' is 50, and similarly for 'I' it is 50. Hence, for 'S', the average is 2500, not 5000. Because 'S' has a square relationship with its parameters. You can see 'S' has a range from 0 to 10000; hence, 5000 might be the expected average value, but it is indirectly 2500 because it is a multiplication of two average values ('L'= 50 and 'I' =50). Therefore, anyone having a score nearby 2500 is a normal person, a score above 5000 is outstanding, and a person having a score between 2500 and 5000 is an above-average candidate.

Remember, one thing: a student of poor intelligence can cover up his success by more labour or hard work, but intelligence alone cannot give you success without hard work. Hence, always stress on labour (hard work) to have a successful career. There is no alternative to hard work, but you have an alternative of intelligence, that is hard work.

As I have mentioned in another part of the book, always quantify the Mehnat (hard work) to assess your performance. Keep a record of your daily study hours or minutes, make a schedule the day before what you are going to study the next day, and strike out whatever is achieved. Note down the highest hours or minutes of daily study and put a star on it if it's a record. Similarly, note down the single-sitting records in minutes and always try to break your own records. You are the only competitor for you. You have to compete with yourself. Try to do better than whatever you have done earlier.

Whenever you count the minutes for daily study or a single study, don't count the minutes of your school classes or coaching classes. Just count the time duration of whatever you are doing in self-study on your own because it is the most effective form of study, which clears your maximum doubts.

For pampered kids, it is very difficult to do hard work because they have entered a comfort zone. Hence, it is very difficult for them to come out of this. The success rate of such individuals is very low because they don't have a tendency to do hard work.

The students who secure the first rank from standard 6th onwards, find it difficult to maintain that rank in Higher Secondary or in higher classes. Hence, a rank of second or third is better than first because the first-rank holders have no one to compete with; they only have to maintain their rank and they cannot have anyone to follow. Hence, it is generally seen that throughout topper of classes 6 to 8, hardly ever topped in the 12th standard or in Civil Services examinations.

05

Reading Summary and Questions First

"The elevator to success is out of order. You'll have to use the stairs, one step at a time."

– Joe Girard

It is quite often seen that there is a fear and reluctance in the minds of students whenever they start reading a new book or any new chapter of any book. Whenever you start a new chapter, it is better to read the questions given at the end of that chapter first; then only you start reading that chapter. If there are no questions at the end, then there is a summary of each chapter in any book; hence, you can read a one-page summary of that chapter. It has many advantages of reading the questions or summary first.

The first is that you will come to know what is given in that chapter. This will create an interest in the chapter by reading only a few questions or only a one-page summary. Another advantage is that after generating an interest in that chapter, your speed will be faster in finishing that chapter. The third benefit is that whenever you encounter the answers to the previously read questions, it will increase your concentration on reading that paragraph or page.

It is a very common feature of books written by foreign authors or printed outside India that the foreign authors always provide a small summary at the end, questions at the end, or at the beginning they mention that "You Will Learn The Following Things In This Chapter." This practice is also found in the notes of IGNOU (Indira Gandhi National Open University) that I read in 1995. On the first page of each chapter, there was a section at the start that said, "You will know in this chapter about," and there were a few questions at the end of each chapter along with a small summary of that chapter.

Another similar but slightly different approach is that if you are appearing in any competitive examination, to read 4-5 years' old questions papers so that it will generate an interest in that chapter or topic.

Also, if you have a detailed syllabus for any examination, it's better to read it before starting to read any topic or chapter. It will create an interest in that chapter and increase your reading speed for that chapter or topic.

I am very much indebted to Mr Anil Jain of the Mechanical branch from Sagar, Madhya Pradesh, who was my batchmate during my engineering degree at SGSITS, Indore, Madhya Pradesh. He gave me the idea of reading questions first and then the chapter later to create an interest in the chapter and increase reading speed.

The above strategy was very useful for me when I appeared in Civil Services examinations in 1996 and 1997, especially when I was reading Schrödinger's equations in Quantum physics and Queueing Theory of mathematics in Operations Research.

06

Revise Previous Class Syllabus

"Success is stumbling from failure to failure, with no loss of enthusiasm."

– Winston Churchill

I have written in other chapters also that there are winners who use their surplus or spare time for some creative work or for studying. During the summer vacation or the winter vacation at Christmas, they utilise their time for some career-oriented work. It is generally heard that many students complete the syllabus of the next year's class during the vacation after the final exam of the current class.

Here, I slightly differ. I suggest that you use this vacation for the revision of the syllabus that you have just read in the previous class. The reason is that when you enter any new class with a new syllabus in a new academic year, it is very difficult to understand everything. But once you have passed that class, you can easily understand everything about each subject. Therefore, it is quite easy to understand everything that you might have struggled with during the year. The revision, which you can do in hardly 15 days, will make your foundation stronger for the next class. After that you can study the subjects of the higher-class syllabus.

Note down the formulae, figures, and details of the previous class syllabus that you may need for the next class so that you do not have to open the books of the previous class every time. More precisely, I recommend reading the subjects that are useful for your career and in which you have an interest. For example, maths, physics, and chemistry for a career in engineering; and physics, chemistry, and biology for medical studies, and arts subjects for humanities students. After reading those, if you have spare time during the vacation, you can also read other subjects from the previous class before moving on to the next year's subjects or syllabus.

It is heard that a student of standard 9th in Kota can solve the integration and differentiation numerical of 12th standard. Don't imitate such guys because they are super outstanding guys who can complete the whole syllabus of 9th to 12th in one year. They are the cream of the whole country. You have to decide your target based on your capacity, not by imitating others.

I will recommend you to complete the full syllabus of 9th and then move to 10th, 11th, and 12th, rather than doing the reverse. Here, again, sequence matters: the choice is yours. Hence, look back and then go ahead.

Always use your previous year's notes and highlighted books for revision because these are very useful in the next year's syllabus for some basic facts and concepts. The Avogadro number's numericals are very useful for higher study as well. Hence, such topics are needed every year for solving numericals in physics and chemistry. So, don't ignore the value of previous year's notes and textbooks.

Generally, coaching classes in Kota teach you the syllabus two years ahead of your class. Hence, normal students who cannot cope with this pressure generally experience depression, and finally, suicidal tendencies come to their mind. Therefore, set targets based on your capacity.

07

Positive Role of Mistakes and Failure

"Education is the most powerful weapon which you can use to change the world."

– Nelson Mandela

There are three things about mistakes for a successful person or winners, i.e. realisation of mistakes, acceptance of mistakes, and correction or rectification of mistakes. The successful candidates learn from their mistakes, and they never repeat such mistakes. If such a mistake is committed by them in their life, first they realise it, then accept it, and finally they rectify it or correct it so that such a mistake will not damage their career in the future.

I am giving some of the real-life examples in which students commit mistakes, and many of them don't want to rectify such mistakes by correcting them.

Many exams that are conducted in hard copy require students to solve multiple-choice questions (MCQs). They often believe they will fill in the choices at the end, but at the end of exams they could not fill in all choices. Therefore, a better strategy is to group questions in sets of ten. After solving each set of ten questions, fill in the corresponding ten answers before moving on to the next set of ten questions. In the worst-case scenario, you may only lose the answers to the last ten questions if the bell signals the end of the exam time. By answering in sets of ten, you can avoid rushing through marking all the answers at the very end, which could result in errors. Hence marking all hundred or two hundred questions at the end in a single stretch may lead to a blunder.

I am just quoting the above example because such type of blunder is committed by many students at the initial phase of their exams. Later, they improve once they realise the mistake.

Another very common mistake committed by students is an error in writing the timetable for exams or misunderstanding the order of the papers. For example, if today's paper is physics but you mistakenly thought it was biology or maths, you will be shocked in the exam hall. This confusion can occur if you either write down the wrong timetable or accidentally read a different date on the correct timetable. To avoid such mistakes, always cross-reference your timetable with 2 or 3 sources. Just after finishing a previous paper, ask two or three students what the next paper is and when it is scheduled. If the upcoming paper is the first one, contact two or three classmates four days before the exam to confirm the subject name, date, and time of the first paper.

Successful candidates always realise the mistake they made. Acceptance of mistake is a very precious virtue of good students. Their nature is not adamant; rather, they are flexible to the changes of time. They acknowledge the mistake and always try to rectify it with a new strategy. Generally, failing students are those who don't accept their mistakes, always hide them, and never try to correct these mistakes.

If your score is poor in any exam or in any subject, don't hide it; instead, tell all your friends about your poor score and accept the reasons why you scored poorly in the exam. Always strive to score better in the next exam. Never create a shield or shelter by claiming that the paper was tough, especially in entrance or competitive exams, because the paper is common to all students and not specifically tough for you.

Generally, it is also seen that the Indian parents hide the failure of their wards and they support such hiding by their kids too. It is because the parents save themselves from the humiliation by the failure of their kids. There is nothing bad in saying that my son or daughter could not perform well in the exam or he or she fails in the exam. If they accept it then next time, he or she will try to do better else he or she will not try to improve. Sometime parents also tell inflated wrong scores of their wards in the competitive exam just to save their own image in the society or neighbourhood.

08

Memory Enhancement by Colour, Music, Perfume

"Your Monday morning thoughts set the tone for your whole week. See yourself getting stronger and living a fulfilling, happier, & healthier life."

– Germany Kent

During my childhood from 1975 to 1985, there were only unique books in the State Board as well as in the CBSE Central Board. The same book was studied across the state in all schools of the State Education Board, and the same book was used or read by generations for years because the syllabus or the pattern was hardly changed in 30-40 years.

Even I remember the chapter or the poem and its colour and photo in my mind, which I read in 1978 in class 1. These will never fade from my memory because our mind or brain captures the snapshots of that page and keeps them for decades, as these were not changing for years.

Today, in the era of computers, every four to five years, the syllabus changes. Chapters are modified, some are deleted, and new chapters are added. Earlier, the books were made using printing presses manually, so they were not changed for years or even decades. However, today, with new machines controlled by computers, it is quite easy to print books by modifying them within a day. Hence, there is no need for offsetting, etc.

Even though the governments have made it compulsory that only approved books of the State Board or NCERT will be taught in class, teachers still recommend many other books as reference materials for students. Even these reference books are also changing their content very frequently because it is quite easy to launch a revised edition of any textbook or reference book.

Hence, today, it is very difficult for the brain of the student to take a snap of the page and save them permanently for decades. So, to face this challenge, it is recommended to read only a few books but have the best book to revise again and again so that you will have a unique picture of each page in your mind. If you use 3-4 colours of highlighter pens and mark the book with different colours, then your mind will take a coloured snap of these pages, and you will be able to recall these pages easily. Always mark with different colours separately for any important traps or tricks whenever you find anything serious or important.

Furthermore, a much better strategy is to create your own notes, especially if you are in a junior class and have enough time to make them. This method will condense a 500-page book into just 200 pages. Since these notes are made by you, it is much easier to remember and revise quickly compared to the 500-page book. In your copy or notes, you will recall the exact position of a paragraph, note, or formula on a page, making it easier to locate information swiftly.

A coloured note or book is easier to remember than a completely black and white mono-coloured notes. Highlighted items are easier to search, and it will not waste your time in finding them.

Apart from colour, our memory is also linked with music, perfume, and the season of the year. Always play mild music whenever you are solving maths problems. Listening to the radio is also a good option during maths study. Whenever you hear that music in the future, you will recall the days whatever you were studying on that day.

Similarly, our memory is also linked with smell. If you inhale a perfume or smell something, after many months, if you smell a similar perfume again, then you will recall the days.

The last is the season of the year, which is also directly or indirectly linked with your memory. You will remember forever what the season was when you were reading biology or physics, when it was raining in that year.

For enhancing your memory, use various sitting positions in your room. In the early morning, study on the bed to revise already read chapters. Sit on a table chair for solving maths with the radio or music on. Sit near the window of the room or use your lawn to study when the climate is good, or go to study on the rooftop or terrace in the evening. If you don't have access to the terrace or lawn, then use your balcony for studying. Change your posture or the place of your study in your home or hostel to enhance your memory or to feel fresh for the next sitting after getting exhausted because it energises you whenever you change your place of study every 2 to 3 hours.

Part II

STUDY EFFICIENTLY

09

Stacking of Books

"One man with courage makes a majority."

– Andrew Jackson

It is a small, minor thing which the student has to keep in mind: how to keep the books or arrange the book so that they can easily be retrieved to read again and again. Always keep the books in a vertical position instead of one over the other, so that it will be easy to take out or replace back. They must be placed in such a position that their names shall be visible without opening each and every book.

If you keep the book one over the other, then your energy will be wasted in taking out any specific book. At the same time, you will be reluctant to take out the lower stacked book, and the use of such a book will be least if it is loaded under other books. Although it is a small thing, it matters a lot for study.

You have to arrange the book in such a way that they are segregated subject-wise in various parts of your almirah in a vertical position, side by side, and their names are visible from outside of the book. These must be easy to take out without shifting or removing the other books.

Arrange books in three styles, depending on their timely requirement. Keep the books of the subject you require immediately nearest to you on a shelf so that you can take out or put back immediately without wasting time. Then come the books you need after a few days or weeks. You can keep such books in another part of the room. The third category, those you hardly need regularly or require once a year or less frequently, you can keep in the loft or another part of the room.

Always keep a few books nearby that are easily accessible, such as a dictionary or formula book, which you need to refer to at least ten times a day. These books should be within arm's reach from your chair.

Always try to stick A4 size paper just in front of the chair on the wall with formulae and values of constants for Maths, Physics, or Chemistry; diagrams; or names for Biology. For Law students and Political Science students, include sections or articles, and for Humanities subjects, add years and other details. These notes on A4 size papers are easy to remember, as you will see them 20 times a day. This way, their images will imprint in your mind for easy recall during your examination.

Generally, the usage of books always depends on their placements, approach, and accessibility. Hence, I conclude:

Never keep your dictionary away from your sitting position; it must be approachable during your study hour from your chair. Never stack your books one over the other otherwise, your lowest book will be the least used for study. It is generally a mental inertia to take out the heavily loaded books placed at the base, and we generally avoid studying such a book. Instead, we use other books rather than the one at the bottom, so finally, we avoid using the lowest stacked book.

You must have racks organised by priority for keeping these books vertically. Keep the books or notes you use daily nearest to you, making them easily accessible. Next, have a rack for books used weekly, and finally, books that you may only use semi-annually or rarely. These less frequently used books can be placed in the loft or similar storage.

10

All Time Ready (ATR) Strategy

"Everything you've ever wanted is sitting on the other side of fear."

– George Addair

It is generally seen that the toppers and the average student both do the hard work almost equally, but a few things make a large difference in results, so that one becomes a winner and the other is reduced to a loser.

Here I am giving a strategy generally adopted by toppers and successful candidates. The successful candidates always believe in the "All Time Ready" strategy. It means they are always ready to appear in any exam, whether it is a multiple-choice question (MCQ) or a narrative-type paper. These toppers keep a slot in the day to revise the old, studied topics; it may be for a few minutes or 1 to 2 hours daily. By revising the already read topics, gives confidence and also clarifies many concepts which they were not able to understand earlier. They remember the formulae or the derivation of many proof-style questions. Hence, they do not need to refer to the books or notes every time they solve the test paper, unlike the average student who opens other books every time to see the formulae, etc., for solving the test paper. It is because of this toppers have good speed and better accuracy in solving test papers.

Because of the confidence mentioned above, the toppers generally select only a few exams to appear in and are fully determined to crack those examinations. Therefore, their attention is solely focused on that one exam; they never waste energy on multiple examinations. They put all their efforts into these selected exams only, and as a result, they become successful. On the other hand, average students appear in multiple exams because they lack confidence in getting selected in a specific exam. The reason for their failure or poor scores is that every exam has its own syllabus and pattern, although it varies slightly. Hence, every time they have to study differently based on the structure of the examination. Due to these multiple examinations, they have to go to various centres to appear in all of them, and it is also quite possible that the exam centres are in different cities or far away from their homes or hostels. Most of their energy is wasted on appearing in various exams to adjust to the pattern and style of the paper.

The average student thinks differently from the toppers. They believe that if they sit in multiple exams, they will be selected in at least one. Therefore, in contrast it is a better strategy to choose a few exams to focus on, give your best in those, and be confident of success in those selected exams. If you repeatedly study the syllabus and practice papers for those specific exams, you will always be prepared for them.

Even if you want to appear in other examinations, choose the most targeted exam and make your full effort for that exam. Don't appear in any other exam conducted before that exam; instead, choose other tests or exams that will be conducted after this paper. Hence, your study will not be affected for the Most Favourite Examination (MFE). I am sure that if you are prepared well for a selected exam, then in that inertia, you can crack other exams also conducted after this exam. After appearing in your Most Favourite Examination (MFE), if you have studied hard for this first and foremost paper, you will be all-time ready for the other exams.

The toppers, I repeat, always make three styles of self-notes depending on how much time they have for the exams. If they have more than three months, they read their detailed notes; if they have only a few days for the exam, they read different pruned notes; and if they have a few hours before the exam, they read only A4 size notes of the formulae, keywords, or tips for answering. These toppers are so well-prepared that by flipping over the pages of the books or the notes, they can recall everything. They can also solve any type of paper, whether multiple-choice questions (MCQ) or the narrative-style paper. It is because of these that they fall into the "All Time Ready" category of successful candidates.

Hence, I want to suggest some tips to average students so that they will also become all-time-ready candidates and finally be the toppers one day.

First, choose only a few exams to appear in and put your 100% effort into those selected exams. Be confident that you will be selected one day in that exam.

Second, revise your whole syllabus, whatever you have read earlier, so that your concept will be clear, and your speed will be enhanced in solving the paper.

Third, always remember formulae, figures, dates, etc., on your fingertips so that you need not refer to other books repeatedly. It will save your time for solving other problems, making you an "All Time Ready" person.

Fourth, make three styles of notes for study based on the duration you have to prepare for the exam. Hence, by revising accordingly, you will be "All Time Ready" for the exam.

Fifth, always target the most desired exam and prepare for that only. Appear in other exams that are scheduled after that; otherwise, you will not be able to give your 100% to your most favourite exam.

Sixth, always flip over the pages of the book or your notes in your idle time or free time every day so that your brain will capture the images of each page in your mind, and you can recall that easily during exams or whenever you need it. Hence, again, you will be the "All Time Ready" guy.

So, there is a thin gap between the approaches of toppers and the average students. Both put in nearly the same effort, but the toppers approach it more strategically and systematically. This difference becomes evident during the results. The outcomes distinguish good students as toppers and the rest as average students.

11

Tendency of Sharing Knowledge

"If you don't risk anything, you risk even more."

– Erica Jong

Generally, students don't know the value of sharing knowledge till they spend their lives at home. But once they join hostel life, they realise the value of sharing knowledge. It is a very common feeling in the minds of students that if they share knowledge, then other students will score better in exams. Or if they share any secret study tips, another student will surpass them.

Such immaturity is there in the mind of every student. I was also not an exception. These are the days when you are generally in classes below Higher Secondary or High School. But once you join Engineering or Medical college or any other degree course, then you start realising the value of teamwork, group study, or comradeship in life.

During the hostel days, when you are far away from your parental protections and care, these fellow students help you in day-to-day life. This is the initial phase of sharing knowledge; here you make various friends for group study before exams. They help each other, and their little bit of help to each other results in smoothly passing exams and solving many tough problems that otherwise could not be solved individually.

Such types of sharing of knowledge are more prevalent when living in a shared room occupied by two or three students rather than in a single-seated room. Hence, it is better to opt for a double-seated shared room than a single-seated room. At the same time, having too many room partners can be detrimental to studying; therefore, double or a maximum of triple sharing rooms are preferable. Choose a room partner who has a similar nature or habits to yours. If you are an early riser, then select someone who is also an early riser. Similarly, if you study late at night, choose a person who also studies late at night, not vice versa.

Always choose a study partner who is more intelligent and hardworking than you. This way, you can learn better reading habits and some effective study techniques. Through their hard work, you will also be motivated to increase your study stamina.

I want to give a simple illustration of how teamwork or a group can enhance your knowledge. The condition is that every person in the group must have the same tendency to share knowledge, and they are willing to share their knowledge with each other.

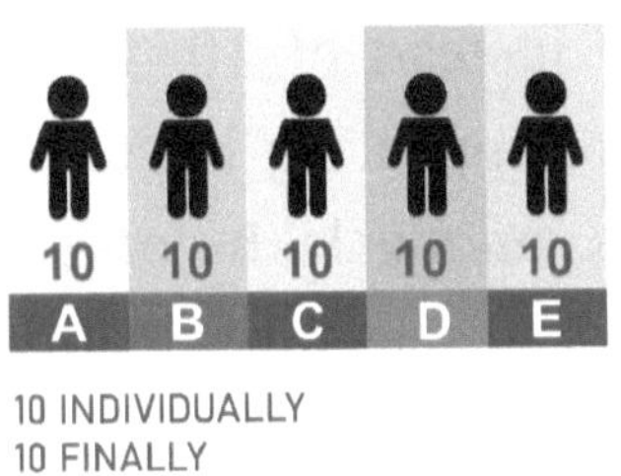

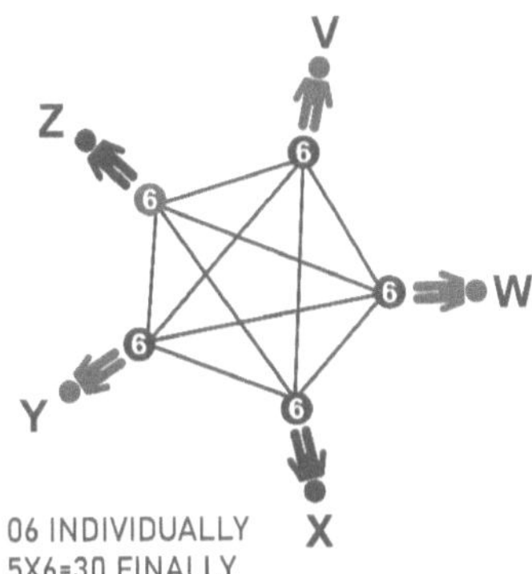

In group 1, there are five persons: A, B, C, D, and E, who are more knowledgeable. Each one of them has ten pieces of information or tricks individually, but they are not sharing their knowledge with each other. At the same time, there is another group, group 2, of five persons: V, W, X, Y, and Z, who are less knowledgeable having only 6 pieces of information but have a tendency to share their knowledge with each other.

Hence, as a net effect, even though in group 1, everyone is more knowledgeable than the other groups' guy, their knowledge is limited to ten individually. In group 2, each one has six pieces of information, which is less than the first group's individual knowledge. However, due to sharing this knowledge, the total information each individual in the second group possesses will be 30, triple the information held by each member of the first group.Hence, you can see that in group 1, the final result is the same because each student is living in isolation in his own silo and not mixing with each other, and not sharing their knowledge. They are limited to whatever they have. In group 2, you can see that by sharing knowledge, less intelligent persons become more informative and knowledgeable.

If the group 1 had shared knowledge, their individual information would have been 50 instead of 10. Hence, try to share your knowledge if you are appearing in competitive examinations. The competition is among lakhs of students, and there are many seats, not just one seat for selection. You might be thinking that by sharing knowledge or information, the other person will be selected, and you will be out of the race.

If you have the tendency of sharing knowledge, then only other guys will also share their knowledge. Here you have to give first, then only in return you will receive something. Don't put a precondition that when someone gives me information, then only I will give in return. Be a big-hearted person and donate whatever you can; in return, you will get manifolds. It is because of that many study centres have developed in various parts of our country such as in Delhi, Patna, and Allahabad for competitive exams like IAS, etc.

Centres in Delhi include Jia Sarai, Ber Sarai, Mukherjee Nagar, and Rajendra Nagar. Other cities such as Allahabad and Patna also have similar centres, and the success rate in these cities and areas is much higher than in any other part of the country.

I want to give real-life examples that happened in my life:

We were living in Jia Sarai, preparing for the Civil Services examination in 1996. My next-door neighbour, Mr. Harish Ahuja, and I were both taking the exam. One day, he came to me and said, "Deepak, there is a solution book available for the past five years' Physics papers in the market, and people are saying it's very good." At that time, I was not aware of this book, so I went to Jawahar Book Depot in Delhi and bought it; it cost hardly Rs 200. Harish was also taking the Civil Services examination, with Mechanical and Maths as his optional subjects, while mine were Physics and Maths.

After reading previous years' solutions to questions, I was able to solve many Physics questions. The confidence I gained from solving those questions enabled me to tackle similar ones from other books. Harish has been selected in the Civil Service examination twice and also in the IES (Engineering Services examination). Finally, he joined DANICS (Delhi, Andaman Nicobar Island Civil services). He is an outstanding person with a polite nature.

When I appeared in the Civil Service examination of 1997 for Physics paper in November, I found that two questions were repeated from the previous year's papers. The first was on Magnetism, and the other was on the Theory of Relativity. I started answering the exam from the Magnetism question, in which I was confident.

The answers were so perfect that I got good marks in Physics paper. Thanks, Harish, for helping me without expecting anything in return. I am just giving the example so that you will learn the value of sharing knowledge or information.

A small but valuable piece of information given by Harish was very useful to me. It has changed my life by helping me score better in Physics. You can also find hundreds of Harish in your life, or you can become a Harish for many of your colleagues.

Similarly, for Maths, Essay, and General Study, we also formed a group of three people: Arvind Dubey, Manish Malviya, and I (myself). Arvind Dubey later got selected in MPPSC and joined as DSP, while Manish Malviya is in IES (Indian Engineering Services, and finally, he was allotted Indian Ordnance Factory Service, IOFS). We used to exchange Maths, General Study and Essay questions with each other to solve within a limited time, just to recreate the examination environment. Thanks to this practice, I was able to achieve better scores in Maths and Essay in the Civil Service examination.

Hence, it is you who can find friends like Harish Ahuja, Arvind Dubey, and Manish Malviya, but at the same time, your nature shall also have the tendency to share your knowledge with them.

Finally, I want to give one last example:

During my Engineering Degree, there was one of my seniors, Mr. Ajay Jadia, who suggested me a very good book of English. The book was "Word Power Made Easy" written by Norman Lewis. I bought that book for thirty rupees during my hostel life in Indore, and I read the book fully in 30 days because I was slow in reading English. As I just started reading English after entering Engineering college, before that, my medium of education was Hindi. The book was very helpful, and I really want to thank my senior, Mr. Ajay Jadia, for suggesting me that book.

Sharing knowledge creates a win-win situation for every candidate in the group. No one is a loser in this game, which is beneficial to all. You learn the good things and good ideas of others, and others also learn the good things of yours. It is also certain that if someone does not share their knowledge, then other students will come to know about their nature, and they will keep that person away from their group. Hence, keep sharing knowledge. So, share the knowledge and have a good friend circle or live in isolation in your own silo like a frog: The choice is yours.

12

Maintaining a Diary

A good diary is required for proper assessment of study so that you will see the improvement in the last few months, and you will try to further increase your study hours. If you are not able to afford a good diary, then use a long-size copy having nearly 150 to 200 pages. The purposes of the diary are multiple; it can be used for record keeping of your daily study hours plus any record you make or break for a single study sitting. Whenever you make or break any daily study hours records or single sitting study records, then mark a star at that line.

Another use of a diary is to keep a daily new page for books or chapters you have to read the next day and an hourly schedule for that day. Whenever you complete that target, strike out that item from the list and note down the sitting duration in minutes. Add them for each day. Here, again, you mention a star if you break or make any record for a full day of study. It will inspire you to study more the next day, and you will always try to break the previous record and make a new record of daily study hours. Also, note down the books or subjects you have to finish in targeted days on a separate page. Then, whenever you finish that book or subject, strike it out and note down the date when you finished it and the duration in days to finish that book or subject.

Now compare the number of the days in which you completed that book or subject with the target days you have given for completing that. If it is finished in the allocated days, then good enough, but if you finish it before the due date, then very good. Now you can further tighten your target for the next book or subject. The last is if your book or subject could not be completed in the desired days, then either you have to set a realistic target as per your studying capacity, or you have to increase your study hours or speed. The diary is your mirror or your report card. By just reviewing it, you can see your improved performance or you can see your shortfall in your efforts. It will daily inspire you to do better than your previous day's performance, and you will always try to make the record and to break the previous ones.

The diary can also be used to note down the dates of various exams and the last date of filing up forms for them. You can also note down the username and password for various examination sites so that you will not forget your user ID or password; otherwise, you will waste your precious time just before the examination trying to retrieve your account ID or password.

The diary can also be used to note down any problems that you cannot solve by yourself and for which you need help from your teachers and friends, or to write any paragraph you are not able to understand and need clarification from your class teachers or colleagues.

13

Night Planning for Next Day

It is always better to plan for the study of the next day before going to bed. Spend at least 15 minutes before night sleep and plan the study for the next day morning onwards. Make an hourly schedule for the next day from early morning to late at night. Choose the most interesting subject to start at, let's say, 4 o'clock in the morning. The grasping power is at its peak in the morning when you wake up; hence, choose a subject that requires remembering minute details, like theoretical lessons or chapters.

Avoid solving maths questions or numerical type questions in Physics, Chemistry, etc. The initial 2 hours of the new day, is good to remember these theoretical subjects then after 2 hours choose the subject like maths or numerical type of questions so that after reading of exhaustive subject initially for 2 hour these numericals will again refresh your mind to grasp the new subjects. Always take 5 minutes break between the two studies.

The hourly pattern shall be as follows:

Time	Subject/Topics	Remarks
4 to 6 a.m.	History, Biology, Physics (Not Numerical or Maths)	
6 to 8 a.m.	Numerical or Maths	

Time	Subject/Topics	Remarks
8 to 9 a.m.	Daily routine: toilet, brushing, bath, or breakfast.	
9 to 11 a.m.	Chemistry, or any second subject	
11:30 am to 1:30 pm.	Another subject	
1:30 to 2:00 p.m.	Lunch	
2 to 4 p.m.	Rest, sleep, or power nap in the afternoon.	
4 to 6 p.m.	Third Subject	
6:15 to 7:45 p.m.	General Knowledge for CSE or any Subject for JEE/NEET.	
7:50 to 8:50 p.m.	Numerical.	
9.00 to 9:30 p.m.	Dinner	
9:30 to 10:30 p.m.	Another subject	
10:40 p.m. to 12 midnight	Any interesting topic, so that you will not feel sleepy.	

Such types of schedules have to be made before going to bed so that your target is fixed for the next day on what to do. Whenever you achieve it, then strike it out so that you will feel like the mission is completed for that slot. It will give you great happiness, and this "Strike Out" will encourage you to read the next subject of the given time slot.

Always start the study with the most interesting subject or topic for you. Similarly, finish the study at night with the most interesting topic, and you have to keep other non-interesting or less interesting subjects in between. The reason is that if you choose a less interesting topic to read in the morning, then you will feel sleepy and there is a higher probability of going back to bed to sleep again. Similarly, for the night, you have to choose the most interesting topic to finish off your study for that day.

If you choose a good topic of your interest to study in the morning, then you will feel energetic in getting up the next day because all night you will anticipate waking up early to read that interesting topic, leading to a relaxed night's sleep.

If during your studies you feel that the topic is not interesting and is leading you towards depression, then change the subject or topic immediately. Take a break for at least half a day or a full day to watch a good inspirational or comedy movie. This way, you will either feel motivated or lighter.

Don't study many subjects all together; it's better to choose 2 to 3 subjects for daily study. Once you finish any one of these, then only switch over to a new subject. Otherwise, reading multiple subjects in a day reduces your speed and quality of your study.

Always note down the total number of minutes of your study whenever you finish your time slot for any topic. Always sum that up after the completion of your daily study; it will range from 480 to 720 minutes, or even more.

Note down two records of your study. The first is the longest duration of a single sitting in minutes; it may range between 120 to 180 minutes. The other record is the highest number of minutes studied in a full day, ranging between 540 to 720 minutes. Whenever these records are broken, you will feel happy and will try to set a new record by surpassing the old one in either category. The purpose of maintaining these records is to increase your study stamina and motivate you to study hard.

Remember the most important thing: you have to dedicate one hour daily to revise whatever you read the day before.

This way, the revision will imprint those pages or chapters permanently in your mind. Hence, recalling becomes easier whenever you revisit that topic, and it also clears many doubts that were not resolved during your initial study or reading. Therefore, even the revision of summary of the previous day's study is very important.

14

Light Up Agarbatti for Longer Stretch

"The road to success, and the road to failure, are almost exactly the same."

– Colin R. Davis

I t is a method adopted by me to study in a single sitting without interruption. I used to light an incense stick (agarbatti) that burned for 60 to 75 minutes. When I was in Jia Sarai in Delhi, the easily available agarbatti was "WOODS" of Cycle brand, which lasted for 75 minutes. During its burning time, I never left my chair, which helped increase my study stamina. The freshness and aroma of the agarbatti in the study room create a good ambience and are always linked to our memory. Students who are allergic to smells or smoke, or who have asthma, should avoid it and not burn it in a closed room. Light up at least two agarbattis daily, one in the morning and one in the evening, as an offering to God. Doing this during prayer will fill you with positive energy and keep you away from depression. You can increase the use of agarbatti to enhance your study stamina based on your financial capacity and preferences.

By burning the agarbatti and paying obeisance to God, or meditating for 15 minutes, you can keep negative energy at bay.

Burning agarbatti is beneficial for concentration, but always keep it away from your table or seating area. The mild aroma of the essence is helpful for enhancing your memory power and refreshing your mind. This is based on my personal experience; others may have different opinions. You can decide based on your nature and preferences. However, excessive use is always harmful, so avoid it if you feel uncomfortable.

15

Draining Out of Energy: Recharging Cycle

"Our greatest glory is not in never falling, but in rising every time we fall."

– Confucius

There is a limit to study hours in a single sitting because our mind and body get exhausted. Study drains our energy, so it requires recharging the mind and body by giving them a sufficient time interval between two studies. We have productive and non-productive tasks in our daily routine.

The productive works for study cover reading, writing, revising old notes, reading newspapers, and remembering already studied topics. The other one is called non-productive work for study. They are tasks done during the intervals between productive study tasks. These include natural calls, brushing, bathing, having breakfast, lunch, dinner, playing games, and watching TV, etc.

These non-productive works are used as recharging slots for the body and mind. Hence, if you get exhausted in productive works for study (like revision or study), then these intervals give you a fresh energy for reading again so that, overall, you can study 10 to 12 hours daily for competitive exams.

The following diagram shows how these intervals can be used to recharge your body and mind.

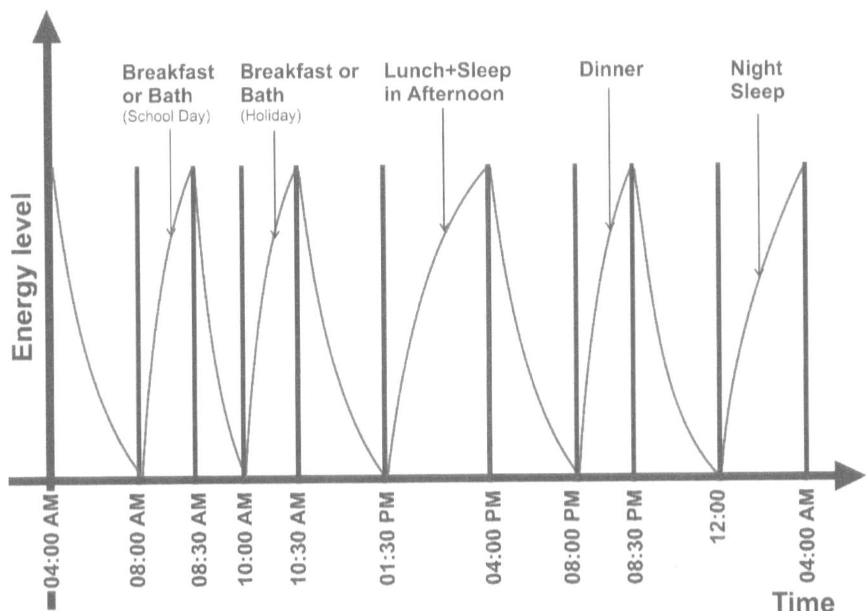

The most effective among these are the power nap in the afternoon, lasting 2 hours, and a complete full night's sleep of 8 hours.

Sequence Matters:

Study, then play, or play, then study.

I prefer the first one, "Study then play." The play covers any games, whether outside, indoor, or watching TV, etc. Study is an activity that requires effort, but play is effortless (unless you are a world-class sports person). Therefore, we should finish the study first, which requires effort, and then move on to effortless activities (such as playing games or watching TV) because it will happen automatically. It recharges you for further study.

But if we choose "Play then study," the second option, then there will be smoothness in playing games. However, it will be very difficult to start the study afterwards because the body will be completely exhausted and partially your mind too. There will be a reluctance in starting study after playing the games.

Generally, the students adopt the second method of study, but for competitive examinations, they have to switch over to the first pattern, "Study then play." This is because the difference between both patterns lies in effort and effortless action. I am mentioning some tips for reducing energy drain or speeding up your recharging cycle.

The first one is that if you are an early riser, then at 4:00 a.m. and after dinner at 9:00 p.m., study only the most interesting topics; otherwise, you will feel sleepy.

Secondly, enhance memory by changing your sitting position in the room or house. By varying your posture while sitting, you can boost memory and improve study stamina. Memory is also enhanced by using different colours of pens, markers, or highlighters to emphasise notes or books. Therefore, always use multi-coloured pens to make recalling easier during examinations.

During reading or studying, seeing natural light from a window and studying from darkness to sunlight (rising sun) is a good experience. It also enhances your memory, and I suggest you sit in a place where you are facing a window for the natural light that comes after sunrise.

Suppose you started studying at 4 o'clock in the morning and sit facing the window of your house, hostel, or room. Then, the transition from darkness to natural sunlight will give you a very refreshing feeling and enhance your memory.

Another good tip is the rooftop study. If you have access to the roof in your hostel or house, you can study there until dusk. Use notes or books to revise during this time slot; generally, it is from 5:30 p.m. to 7:00 p.m. depending on the season. Sitting in an open space and studying in natural light is an amazing experience. It can recharge you and enhance your memory.

16

Inspirational Speeches, Movies, Books or Quotes

"Opportunities don't happen, you create them."

– Chris Grosser

In every country and in every language, there are many movies made every year, which are very motivational and inspiring. These are in the fields of sports, education, corporate world, etc. I want to quote a few of them: *Chak De*, *3 Idiots*, *The Karate Kid*, and recently *12th Fail*.

Every such movie has a learning lesson in it, which can motivate you to do better and further better for your success. Similarly, there are many motivational books written every year. You can read these books so that you will be inspired to achieve your target. A good book, although not motivational, which I read in 1991, was suggested by my senior, Mr. Ajay Jadia. The book was "Word Power Made Easy" authored by Mr. Norman Lewis. This book was very useful for my English foundation. Another one was "You Can Win" by Mr. Shiv Khera, and the latest one is "Rich Dad Poor Dad" by Mr. Robert T. Kiyosaki.

Apart from these movies and books, there are some inspirational speeches or motivational talks by motivational speakers which you can find on YouTube. There are quotes by great leaders and successful individuals. Did you notice the inspirational and motivational quotes just before each chapter of this book?

Such movies, speeches, books, and quotes not only inspire and motivate you but can also help save you from falling into depression and suicidal tendencies.

Always watch or read some stories or series of achievers; these are called "Achiever's Series." Such movies, books, reels, or videos you should watch or read once. The best ones, you have to watch or read repeatedly. So, whenever you feel depressed, try to read or watch such books or movies.

Part III

FACING EXAMS

17

Speed Graphs in Exams

"No one changes the world who isn't obsessed."

– Billie Jean King

Here I am comparing the two patterns generally followed by the students. The first graph Graph 1, shows the speed and accuracy of solving the questions by the average student, and the second one, Graph 2, is followed by the toppers.

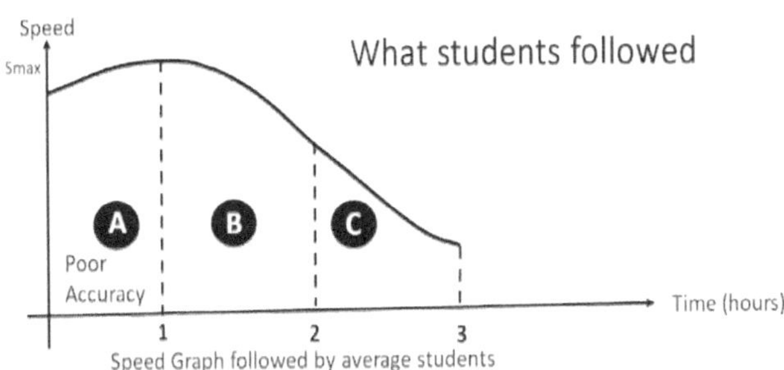

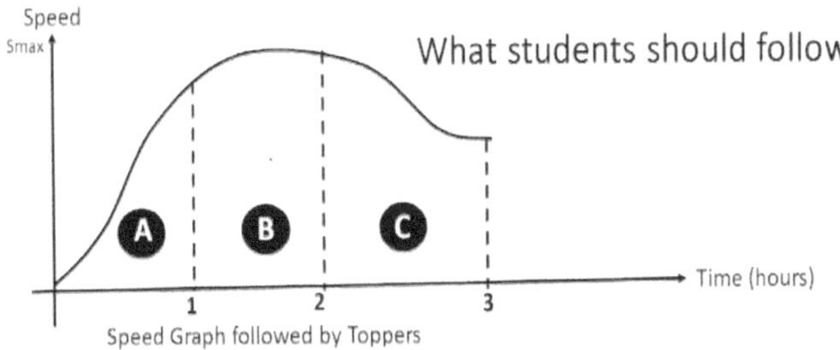

Graph 1: What is generally followed by students.

Here, the graph shows the speed of solving questions on the Y-axis and on the X-axis, it represents the time or duration of the examination. I have taken an average of 3 hours just to explain the pattern. There are generally two types of question papers: Multiple-choice questions (MCQ) and narrative, essay or subjective types of questions.

A. Multiple choice questions (MCQ)

It is generally seen that a normal or average student follows a unique pattern of solving paper in the first hour of an exam. They try to solve immediately without considering the accuracy of the correct answer. They start with their highest speed initially and keep thinking about solving the whole paper, possibly incorrectly. Due to the very high speed, they realise that their answers do not match the given 4 choices (A, B, C, or D). Then, they rush to another question with the same high speed. Again, they encounter the same issue with this question, so they switch to yet another one, still at their highest speed. After attempting these 4 to 5 questions with high speed and poor accuracy, and finding their answers don't match the given answers, they generally feel depressed. However, they refuse to compromise on their speed and continue solving at a high pace, resulting in finishing their paper with poor speed and accuracy.

B. Narrative-type questions

Here again, the aspirants of Civil Services and state PSC (Public Service Commission) and of other exams, whenever replying to the subjective answer, generally start writing the answer at their highest speed initially. When they start writing at their highest speed, their handwriting becomes illegible, and the evaluator cannot read it clearly. Hence, the impression he carries for checking the balance paper is generally very poor. Here the first answer impresses the evaluator in two ways: first, by good handwriting and another by good contents of the answer. Because of the very high speed in the very first question, the aspirants spoil the handwriting. Additionally, in the subsequent questions, they maintain the same speed.

They never give time to read the instructions given at the top of the question paper. They never read the full question paper before starting to attempt the best-known question first. They never structure the answer to any question. The only thing they keep in mind is that there is a shortage of time, and they have to finish it within the time given, even if with imperfect or wrong answers and poor handwriting. After answering imperfectly and with poor handwriting, they get depressed during the first hour of the exam. Even then, they continue with that high speed, poor handwriting, and unstructured answering.

Graph 2: What should students generally follow.

This is the graph generally followed by the toppers or the successful candidates. They generally target the part A of the graph to give their best, and in that inertia and confidence, they perform better in parts B and C of the graph. This is the graph or pattern every student has to follow because it is the best optimum graph to get the best efficiency and accuracy in solving questions.

A. Multiple-choice questions (MCQ)

Generally, toppers take more time for solving the initial 4 to 5 questions patiently. Once they solve these questions correctly, they find that their answers match with one of the options given in the multiple-choice questions. This encourages them to solve the next question with more accuracy but slightly higher speed compared to the previous questions. Therefore, in every subsequent question, their speed increases along with the accuracy. These initial few questions in part A of graph 2 encourage them to perform better and faster. By the end of part A of graph 2, they achieve the maximum speed in solving questions. However, such toppers never compromise on accuracy to increase their speed in solving papers. Even at the end of the exam, they maintained almost the highest speed in solving the paper.

Hence the toppers maintain the accuracy of answering in the whole exam period but they enhance the speed gradually in reaching the maximum speed after few minutes unlike the average students who try to attain the highest speed initially with imperfect answers.

B. Narrative type questions.

Generally, top students read the instructions of the question paper first in a few seconds. Then, they read the questions in a few minutes and search for the best-known question. They start answering with this best-known question first. After choosing this question, they take some time to structure the answer. They create a rough draft in their mind and, after pondering for 2 to 3 minutes, they start writing the answer patiently with their best handwriting. This first question, both in content and handwriting, leaves an impression on the evaluator, which influences the assessment of the rest of the paper. Therefore, it is always advised to frame, structure, and write the first answer in the best possible way and handwriting. Choosing the first question to answer is also an art in examinations.

Hence, I am suggesting the following tips to attempt the papers.

1. First, for narrative questions, read the instructions first, in a few seconds, and then read the whole paper. If it is a subjective paper, choose the first question patiently to answer. Take 2 to 3 minutes to make a draft answer in mind and note down the main points to cover in the answer. Then start writing in good handwriting slowly, without any correction or mistake. After writing 2-3 pages, you can increase your speed without compromising on your handwriting and without any correction or mistakes. Finish the paper at least 10 minutes before the exam duration to just go through the answers again and make corrections or add-ons if needed.

2. Second, for multiple-choice questions (MCQ) also read the instructions first, then try to attempt the chapter in which you are confident, if your system permits choosing the chapter and you have the option available to go to the section of your choice. In a few exams like GMAT, there is no option to go to the desired section; you have to solve the questions in the order they appear. Hence, after choosing the section of your choice, take more time to solve the first question with full accuracy. If you can solve it well, good; if you are not able to solve it in two to three attempts, then skip to the next question after marking the probable answers on a rough page indicating the question number. Keep on solving 4-5 questions patiently, then enhance your speed. By solving

these four or five questions correctly even though in a longer time duration, you will get a confidence in solving further questions, and after 20-30 minutes, you will reach your maximum speed of solving paper that too with full accuracy. The inertia of accurate answering 4 to 5 questions leads you to solve the paper completely and with higher accuracy. Never try to go with highest speed for solving 4-5 questions initially, it will be a blunder. Hence enhance your speed gradually with higher level of accuracy throughout the paper.

18

70:20:10 Strategy

"Keep your eyes on the stars and your feet on the ground."

– Theodore Roosevelt

70:20:10 is a general pattern of questions in every examination. Here, we have grouped the questions based on toughness into three categories. There are 70% questions that are very normal, and a student of normal or average prudence can solve them. The next 20% can be solved by an intelligent student, and the last 10% of questions are the toughest, meant for very outstanding students.

In the diagram given, you can see that if a person goes from 70% to 20% and then finally to 10% questions, the progression or ride is very smooth for them. However, if they start from 10% to 20% and finally to 70%, then it becomes a blunder, even for an outstanding student. Here, once again, the sequence or order matters, and the choice is yours.

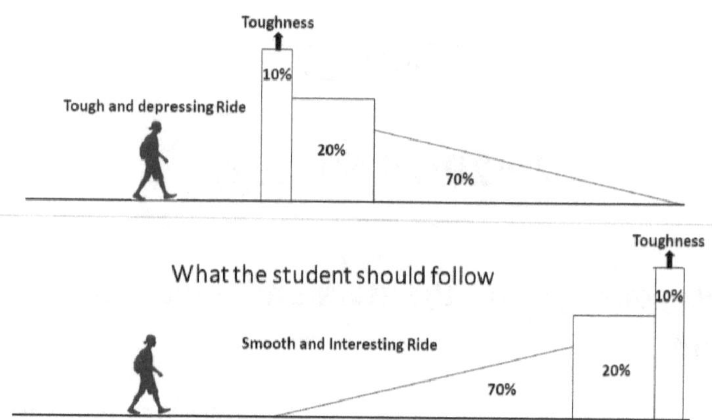

I am stressing upon this sequence of 70:20:10 strategy because the cause of every suicide lies here, and we have to tackle the root cause of depression and suicidal tendency among students. Generally, almost all the students target this 10% first and then want to move to 20% and finally to 70%. It is a very dangerous strategy, and students generally fall into it. Even if an outstanding student targets 10% first, there is a higher probability that he will go into depression and perform very poorly in examinations.

Hence, for better scoring in exams, I am providing a more reasonable strategy for tackling it, based on 70:20:10. The students should target 70% of the questions and solve them repeatedly. Once they have solved the 70% many times, they will then be able to tackle the next 20% with inertia and confidence because the concept or foundation of solving this 20% will lie in the 70% of questions. Therefore, when you have mastered the 70% and 20% (i.e. a total of 90%), you should then switch over to the remaining 10%. Here is where the role of cross-subsidisation of time comes into play.

Cross-subsidisation is a term used in Economics and Commerce for the costing or pricing of any commodity or service. Some products or services are sold at a lower price to attract customers, subsidising the less affluent individuals by selling at a reduced profit or at a loss. This shortfall is compensated for by selling other services or products at higher prices to premium customers.

You can see that in airfare for Business and Economy class, and in the railway in AC versus Non-AC class passenger, here in the railway, the losses of the general or non-AC class are covered from the AC classes.

Similar approach of cross-subsidisation can be adopted in solving papers in examinations. The time saved from solving 70% of the questions can be used to tackle 20% of the questions, and then the remaining time can be allocated to attempting the remaining 10%, which are designed for exceptional students. The 70:20:10 solving pattern should be practised at home when working on test papers because after practising the 70% and 20% sections multiple times, you will find the last 10% much easier to solve. Remember the sequence 70:20:10 to avoid mistakes. While solving the last 10% directly is suitable for exceptional students, but they should first master the 70% and 20% sections before attempting the toughest 10%.

In Kota, it is generally seen that coaching classes are chasing that 10%, hence only a few outstanding students can cope with the pressure, and this outstanding lot brings the name to the coaching. Hence, the primary focus of these coaching classes is the **"99 percentile and above"** scoring students.

These coaching classes classify students in various batches like star batches, droppers' batches, average students' batches etc. But when a student, who initially admitted to a star batch and then moves down to lower grade batches, goes into deep depression. This is because he feels insulted and thinks that his career is devastated, and finally, he will be out of the race for the best engineering or medical colleges. Adoption of this strategy of 70:20:10 by students and timely counselling by teachers can prevent many cases of depression and suicide in Kota every year.

Another similar trap I want to quote for the students who are appearing in Civil Services examination. In the Prelims Paper of the Civil Services examination, one question was asked: which snake makes its own nest? After reading this question in 1994, an interest was generated in my mind for reading biology books of B.Sc. so I borrowed one book from my younger sister, Sangeeta, who was living in Panna. I then read about all the types of snakes found across the world. After 10 days, I realised that I could not recall any snake with its features. There are many such misleading questions in examinations. Paper setters also test your capacity to eliminate. How easily can you find out what is relevant or irrelevant? It was a good lesson for me to learn to ignore whatever I cannot remember for long. These are exceptional questions asked rarely, and they will not be repeated again.

Another similar question was asked in the Prelims of the Civil Services examination, which was: which darbari (Royal members of the court of the emperor) saw the reigns of seven emperors during the medieval period of Indian history? Such types of questions cannot be found in history, and the answer cannot be seen directly in any book. By reading such questions, we generally get diverted and start studying differently by modifying our strategy. These are exceptional occurrences; hence, don't chase such questions too much. Rather, target the 70%, then the 20%. Such questions about snakes or darbari are hardly less than one percent; hence, invest your energy in the 99% rather than in random 1% questions.

A similar strategy was adopted by me in standard 6th to 10th for remembering the Roop (Balak-Balko-Balkah) and Dhatu Roop (Aham-Vayam, etc.) in sanskrit. These were consuming a lot of time of my study, hence it was very difficult to compromise on my other subjects of interest like maths, physics, chemistry, and biology. Even within sanskrit, I didn't want to lose 84% at the cost of this 16%. Hence, I never remembered or read the Roop or Dhaatu Roop in sanskrit. My score was always forty-two marks out of 50, and the eight marks which were lost every year because of Roop and Dhaatu Roop. But I was happy because the remaining 42 marks gave me distinctions every year, and the choice was mine.

For targeting 70%, you need only the basic textbooks and read them many times. Once you get expertise in that, then only move to some reference book for cracking 20% and then 10%. But it is seen that students first go for multiple reference books instead of reading basic books. For targeting 70%, the books of NCERT are perfect basic books, and physics by Resnick and Halliday is a good book for the concept of physics. After finishing such basic books, you have to move to other reference books, that too after mastering the basic conceptual books.

Hence, I want to conclude that you should not directly jump to 10%, rather hone your skill in 70%, then 20%, and finally go to 10%. Never attempt the toughest questions or chapters first; start with the easier ones. Don't worry about the 10%. First target 90%, and then the 10% will come automatically.

19

Strategy for Replying or Answering in Examinations

"Failure is simply the opportunity to begin again, this time, more intelligently."

– Henry Ford

It is seen that students try to solve the question paper quickly in competitive examinations, and in that flow, they make some mistakes in the initial 10 to 15 minutes. These few initial wrong answers lead them to feel demotivated during the exam within 30 minutes of the commencement of the examination. There are two types of strategies: one for multiple-choice questions and another for lengthy or essay-type questions.

For multiple-choice questions (MCQs), invest triple the average time allotted for each question to solve the first few questions, and then a little less time for the next question. This approach can increase your accuracy. You may find that by the fifth or sixth question, you can solve it in a fraction of the average time given for each question in the examination. Today, almost all papers are online for examinations like CAT, GMAT, GRE, SAT, NEET, or JEE. In some examinations like GMAT, you cannot jump to the next question until you solve the previous one. However, in many other exams or hard copy exams, you can move to the last question before solving the previous one. Therefore, focus on the topics or questions on which you have full command, with 100% accuracy and good speed in solving them.

For the essay or subjective type of question paper, solve the best-known question in any competitive exam, as it creates a first impression in the mind of the evaluator.

If you are appearing in an essay-type examination like in UPSC's CSE Mains, then if you have three hours for one essay (like during my time in 1996), don't start writing immediately. Take 15 minutes to choose the best topic for writing the essay, then spend 30 minutes making the structure or body of the essay. After that, utilise 120 minutes for writing it and, finally, spend 15 minutes for proofreading or making some additions.

During hard copy exams or online exams, in which you can skip the questions, if you encounter questions where you are unsure between two answers, for example, A and C both appearing correct but you are uncertain about the perfect answer, note down the question number and the possible answers as A or C. Skip to the next questions. Similarly, for other questions with similar confusion between two answers, make a list of 3 to 4 such perplexing questions with their possible answers. Proceed to solve the remaining paper. After completing the rest of the paper, revisit these questions, considering only the probable answer. Here, you can take the risk of choosing either one of the answers if you are unable to decide, especially if there is no negative marking or if answering is mandatory. This approach can save time and increase the likelihood of selecting the correct answer.

The following is an illustration you can understand better: Suppose, during the examination, you find that there are three questions in which you are confused about the exact answer; hence, just note down the question number with probable choices.

13. A or C

45. B or D

63. A or D

Hence, after finishing the whole paper, come to these three questions and re-read them. Even if you are not able to solve them again, take the full risk of choosing either one of them or choose the one which you feel is better than the other.

13. A

45. B

63. D

It has two benefits. First, you need not read the choices of B and D for question number 13. Similarly, for question number 45, you need not read A and C again and finally for question number 63 you need not to read B and C because you have already ruled out them as probable answers and it will save your time. The second benefit is that randomly choosing an answer has a 25% probability of being correct, but here with two options, the probability is 50%. Hence, your probability of a correct answer doubles immediately during the examination for these confusing questions. As the four optional answers of many multiple-choice questions are very lengthy, sometimes ranging from one to two full lines, it saves your precious time during the examination by not having to read the least probable answers again.

If you don't adopt such a strategy for multiple-choice questions, you will have to re-read the whole question and all the answers. This will waste your time, in which time is of the essence, and is very precious in a time-bound examination.

20

Fear and Pressure of Exams: Strategy for Gaps

"The pessimist sees difficulty in every opportunity. The optimist sees opportunity in every difficulty."

– Winston Churchill

For any competitive exams, you have to make a strategy of study by assessing the syllabus and the number of books you have to read to understand the gravity of the exam. If you don't assess the gravity of the exam, then seriousness will not come into your mind, and you will be non-serious about the study.

Firstly, you have to count the number of pages or books and distribute the time to be allotted to each paper based on the weightage of marks for that exam. Devote more time to questions or chapters with more weightage in the exam. A slight fear, tension, or mild mental pressure is needed for the exam so that there will be seriousness in your mind, and you will not be lethargic in your study. Make three styles of notes based on your time availability, as I recommended in other chapters. Always count the days left for your exam. Keep a few days for revision for each paper just before the commencement of the exam.

Don't study too late during your exam days; instead, take a complete 8 to 9 hours of sleep at night so that you will wake up fresh for the final revision the next day. Just stop studying 30 to 40 minutes before your exams and meditate or concentrate by closing your eyes just before the start of your exam while sitting on your chair.

21

Counting of Pages: Reference Book One Only

"A surplus of effort could overcome a deficit of confidence."

– Sonia Sotomayor

For making a target of daily study, you have to assess the minimum number of pages you need to read each day. This minimum count will create pressure on you to be diligent in the days leading up to exams.

Suppose you have 6 to 7 books for study, and each one has 400 pages. The total pages will be approximately 2600. Then you need to study at least three times these pages, so the total pages become 7800. Hence, in one year, you need to study 7800 pages, which also includes revisions. Add any reference book or your notes if you are reading. Then divide this number by the days left for your exam, which is nearly 320 because some days you have to keep for exams and for preparation leave. Here in this case, it comes out to be 24.375; hence, your minimum count is 24.4 pages. These numbers of pages you must read daily.

You can read many books, but for regular study or for revising the topic, always choose the best among these. Apart from that book, you need one more good reference book for study. If you remember many books for the same subject, you may get confused, and your memory will reduce because our mind remembers the picture of each page.

By reading the same topic from many books, doubts can be clarified. However, when it comes to remembering, it may create problems. In such cases, it is better to make self-handwritten notes after reading multiple books on each subject.

I have seen in the case of my daughter that the coaching class teachers referred to many books by different authors, so the total page count came out to be above 18,000 per year. It is just impossible to read the same book again for JEE mains. By reading many books, the kids may get overloaded with study, and it may happen that he studies one topic from five books but leaves many topics untouched before the exam. Hence, the good strategy is to complete the syllabus by reading the best book and then read the selected topic for more clarity from one or two reference books. Remembering or revising from one book enhances your memory, and your mind retains the things as per the picture made in your brain of that page.

Part IV

CHANGE YOUR LIFESTYLE

22

No Time for Love: No Girlfriend or Boyfriend Please

"Just one small positive thought in the morning can change your whole day."

– Dalai Lama

Generally, competitive age starts at 15. This age also marks drastic hormonal changes. It is the age when teenagers start to be attracted to the opposite sex, diverting their minds for sure. This is a natural behaviour. The abnormality lies in not diverting their minds by seeing the person of opposite gender. It is a human nature or even an animal instinct at a certain age. Hence, the issue is, if you are too emotional, then keep yourself away from such love affairs during the age of career formation. You can have a girlfriend or boyfriend if she or he is a driving force or an inspiration for your target, but it is very rare. The chances of your mind being diverted are more of a normal thing than an exception.

You can have another view also, but I recommend that during your study, kindly keep yourself away from such affairs or emotional attachments. Don't waste your time meeting your girlfriend or boyfriend, or talking on the phone; it will divert your mind, and you will find it very difficult to concentrate on your study. Instead, I recommend you make good friends, even of the opposite gender, who can guide you or inspire you for your study or for your mission.

23

Food Habits

"If you can dream it, you can do it."

– Walt Disney

There are a lot of roles of food intake. It is to be full of vitamins and energy. The age of a teenager requires all types of supplements and vitamins because it is the fastest-growing age for body and minds, both, after infancy.

I am giving some of the best food habits for students so that they can follow in their day-to-day lives to have a fit and healthy body and mind. During the age of study, the drainage of energy is very fast, and you need good food to nourish your body and mind both.

You have to take food in such a manner so that there will not be any deficiency of it, which otherwise may invite weakness, headache, or migraine, and at the same time, there will not be any excess intake of it to invite obesity or other ailments.

Generally, it is said that we have to take breakfast like a king, lunch like a prince, and dinner like a pauper. However, for a student's lifestyle, a heavy breakfast may not be practical because it can induce drowsiness by releasing too much sugar into the body. This can make you feel sleepy during your classes or while studying at your table. Therefore, for breakfast, have a fresh apple, a few almonds (preferably soaked in water overnight), a glass of fresh milk, and two biscuits. This constitutes a balanced breakfast. If you like, you can also add some cornflakes to the milk.

By taking this type of breakfast, neither will you feel sleepy in the class or elsewhere due to excess breakfast, nor will you feel weakness or headache due to its deficiency. The time of the breakfast also matters; it must neither be too early nor too late. Hence, you must take it only 2 to 4 hours after waking up and studying a few subjects. The most appropriate time for breakfast is 8:00 a.m. to 8:30 a.m. if you are an early riser.

In lunch, you can have all sorts of vitamins and nutrients. You need to take 2-4 chapatis or rotis made of pure wheat with Daal (pulses) for protein and a small quantity of rice and green vegetables like spinach or gourd. The food at lunch must be in such a way that it releases a sufficient amount of sugar in your body so that it induces a little bit of sleep, and you take at least 2 hours of sleep in the afternoon if you are not in any class or engaged somewhere else. Take another fruit at 6:30 p.m., like pomegranate or banana, for recharging your body after the study slot from 4:00 p.m. to 6:00 p.m. These food intervals and foods not only recharge your body after draining out your energy from studying but also serve as intervals to give your mind fresh energy to study again.

During the dinner, again take an equivalent food as you have in the afternoon, except for the rice. Rice should generally be avoided at night, but if you have the habit of eating rice in the evening, choose your own eating pattern according to your bodily needs.

I am giving the following tips. If you find them useful for your food habits, then please adopt these in your food intake. Otherwise, follow your own diet plan according to your geographical location, trends, and food culture in your family.

- Avoid taking heavy food during exam days.
- Avoid taking food containing Fat, Maida or Nonveg a day before your examination.
- Don't take fast foods or cold drinks or the packaged food rather take fresh lime water with salt and glucose and fresh homemade food.
- Avoid too much spicy and oily food. Take simple food with less oil and spices and avoid too much chilies.
- If you are too much fond of taking nonveg then reduce the quantity of taking it during examination. A day before your exam, also take simple food at night so that you will have a good, relaxing sleep the night before the examination.
- If your exam lasts in two shifts that is in morning and evening, then both are risky. If you are on an empty stomach or if you are taking heavy meals, it's better to take lighter meal, which is good for your health and just sufficient to give you energy for appearing in the exam.

Never ignore the role of milk in the diet; similarly, pulses are needed for proteins. If you don't like milk, then take the curd instead.

If you are consuming too much heavy food, there will be a high release of sugar in your body. Consequently, you will feel tired and sleepy, making it difficult to concentrate on your studies and give your best effort. During student life, your body should be balanced – not too fatty or too lean. Therefore, adopt a diet according to your physique and bodily requirements.

24

Role of Your Friends and Mentors

"He who conquers himself is the mightiest warrior."

– Confucius

There are always role models in your life, like some heroes; they may be your friends, relatives, teachers, parents, etc. You can call them mentors for your life. We encounter such mentors in our life and learn a lot of things, consciously or subconsciously, from these mentors. Generally, they tell many things to you, but you have to remember only a few things that will be useful for your life and can change your future.

There are many good friends who guide you and inspire you. At the same time, there may be many persons who insult you or discourage you, but you have to take both of them positively. If someone insults you or discourages you, then don't feel insulted or insecure. Instead, remember and recall his or her statement daily to inspire yourself. It all depends on you: how you take things. The same statement can inspire you or lead you to a great depression. Always try to work hard so that your bright future will give him or her a befitting reply.

Generally, we are inspired by good people only, but we have to take both good and bad people positively as a source of our inspiration. It is not your argument; rather, your success will speak to them on your behalf, just wait for a good time.

I am a native of Panna (Madhya Pradesh) and I completed my engineering from SGSITS Indore in Electronics and Telecommunication in 1994. Then, I moved to Jia Sarai, Delhi for the preparation of Civil Services examination. I secured all India rank 251 in 1996 in the Civil Services examination and again 218 rank in 1997; both times I got the railway.

During my journey, I met many people who inspired me in my life, whether directly or indirectly, and a few who discouraged or insulted me. I am noting down a few names of those who inspired me or gave me good study tips, which provided me with new hope or light in my life. These will be included at the end of the book in a separate sub-chapter.

I also keep the names in my mind of those who discouraged me or insulted me, but it is a great secret which I don't want to mention. Instead, they are also in my heart because I treat them as a source of inspiration for my small achievements in life.

I am mentioning some of my friends and guides in my life and the issues they have helped me resolve. There are some people who have been a source of inspiration for me. I may not know the exact reasons how they directly influenced the changes in my life, but they have played significant roles in my success.

Although it is not very useful for readers of this book, you can use its analogy in your life to get something from your colleagues, teachers, relatives, etc., that can change your life a little bit positively.

Sister Christina, Headmistress Of Lisieux Anand Vidyalaya, Panna

In 1982, I was studying in class 4 when I was insulted before the whole class by Sister Christina. This was the first incidence in my life where I felt humiliated, and it changed my whole life. Sister Christina was taking a science class at 3:30 p.m., and we three classmates, named Naveen Khairha, Rajaa Mohammad Khan, and I, were talking and whispering in the class, which she had been noticing for the last 10 minutes. Then suddenly, she asked one question: "Which form of water in nature is the purest?"

I replied pond (Taalaab). Naveen replied, "Well" (Kuan), and Rajaa replied, "Canal" (Nahar). Then she asked the same question to Mukesh Jain, and he replied, "Rainwater is the purest form of water found in nature."

Nothing to surprise here that Mukesh was a very outstanding guy; rather, he was just like us, a normal guy, but he was taking tuitions at his home. Mukesh's tutor was teaching three siblings, ranging from 2nd to 6th standard.

The secret of the reply given by Mukesh Jain came to light later when we all visited his home at 7:00 p.m. one evening, while his tutor was teaching all three siblings.

Now I am summarising the incident after the reply of Mukesh Jain, my Principal Sr. Christina (Actually Headmistress but we called her Principal in our small town due to ignorance at that time) told all three of us to get out of the class and fetch two bulls and one gunny bag full of wheat to do farming in the field, which was just in front of my class with some vegetables grown by the school management. After watching the movie "3 Idiots," I recalled that incident in my life. Yes, the chamatkar (miracle) happened on that day in front of 11 girls in our class; all three 'idiots' of that day were standing outside the classroom, observing the field with a well inside it, and fully grown cabbage and cauliflower during that winter.

Sister Christina is still in touch with me. I never forget to wish her on her birthday on 24th July, except once in 37 years. The year when I missed to wish her, she responded in a letter asking how I had forgotten to wish her that year and whether I was okay or not. It was a 10-day delay from my side to wish her because I was busy shifting to my new place of posting. The school used to celebrate her birthday every year, and we used to get one orange toffee on that day after some cultural programme in the honour of her birthday.

I never took that incident as an insult; rather, I took it as an inspiration for my whole life, which later shaped my life for a bright future and career.

25

How You Take Things: Choice Is Yours

"He is a wise man who does not grieve for the things which he has not, but rejoices for those which he has."

– Epictetus

Winners and losers have almost the same road to travel, but the road bifurcates at the end because of their approach to the same thing. The visions of the winners are slightly different from the visions of the losers, even though both are provided with the same types of circumstances and things. There is a thin line gap in the approaches of the losers and achievers. The gap can be of two types: first, winners do things slightly differently, or they walk a little more than the losers do.

It is generally seen that almost all persons follow the winners and seek guidance from successful individuals or achievers. Yes, it is partially a correct strategy, but at the same time, we have to avoid the mistakes committed by the losers in their life. Hence, for perfect and complete success, we have to learn not only "what to do" from the winners but also "what not to do" from the losers. Losers were also winners just before their last step. Sometimes, a small mistake at the end made them losers.

Generally, we use the words "loser" and "winner" for any competition. In my opinion, there are two types of people: those who participated in the race and those who did not. The real losers are those who did not participate in the race. Therefore, those who participated but did not win the trophies or medals are not losers because they have at least taken part in the game and made an effort, even if someone else (the winner) has put in a little more effort.

It is not only the victory, but participation also matters: the second one is the prerequisite for the first one. I am just mentioning these things so that you will start learning how to take the things. Losers and winners, you can learn from both the persons what to do, and one more additional thing from the loser: what not to do.

Every coin has two sides. It depends on you which side you want to take. I am listing some of the things you will come across in your daily life.

If your parents get installed an AC in your room for your study, the AC can give you an additional stamina for studying for three more hours, and at the same time, you can also sleep in comfort. It all depends on you how you make use of the AC provided to you. The choice is yours.

How you take your failure: there are two ways of seeing your failure, either they can inspire you to do better, or they can lead you to some depression. Your success always depends upon how you take your failure in your life.

There are summer vacations after examinations and winter vacations during Christmas. The winners take these days to do something fruitful, but losers engage in some useless activities just to pass the time. The winners learn new things daily in their excess free time.

You have YouTube, Facebook, and WhatsApp on your mobiles. It depends on you whether you are using YouTube for learning new things, Facebook for connecting with great achievers, or just wasting time watching reels and movies on YouTube or WhatsApp, or making girlfriends or boyfriends on Facebook. Your achievement depends on how you utilise these platforms.

You have mobiles and a laptop with internet connectivity. You can use them to search for good information from various sites, or you can use them for watching useless adult movies. The choice is yours.

Your parents give you a new bike just to save your time for going to school, college, or your coaching classes, so that you can use surplus time for more fruitful activities. The same bike you can use for roaming around your city, meeting friends, or you can use spare time to sit in the library to study something.

Your parents give you pocket money. You have two options: you can invest it in purchasing a good book that will benefit your career, or you can throw a party for your friends, or you can spend it on your girlfriend. The choice is yours.

Rich Dad Poor Dad

Rich Dad can be any person having sufficient money, social status, or any good senior officers or well-placed person in any company who can afford anything you desire. You can use his wealth in either way. His assets can inspire you to further increase his empire. You have a separate room with AC fitted in it and an attached bathroom with all sorts of luxuries and comforts. You can use these luxuries and comforts to increase your study hours in a non-interfering ambience. Now comes how you take the things.

You have all the luxuries of your life; hence, either you can inspire yourself to further increase them and expand your empire, or you can just enjoy life because you have all the luxuries of life; hence, you have no ambitions to achieve anything further. The choice is yours.

Poor dads are those who have barely enough money for immediate needs. They live hand to mouth, hardly having any surplus money or social status, or any luxuries for their kids. Here, again, their poverty can inspire their kids to achieve something in their lives, or it can lead them into depression. The kids can think about breaking the shackles of poverty by working hard and studying diligently, or the same poverty can break their determination. Sometimes, the inferior job of a poor dad inspires his kids more than the superior job of a rich dad does.

Generally, it is felt that a poor kid has to work harder to achieve success in life than a rich kid, but in reality, the rich kid is also under tremendous pressure because the poor kid has everything to achieve. He has nothing to lose; whatever he does, either he will gain something or lose nothing. A rich kid has to adopt a two-pronged strategy: to expand the empire and not to lose the existing one. Hence, the challenges before the rich kids are equal or even more compared to what poor kids have.

Doing 10 to 12 hours of study for a rich kid is very difficult because he is a pampered kid with full of luxuries and comforts. Hence, every year it is proved by the Civil Services examination's results that it is very difficult for the son or daughter of an IAS officer to become an IAS; rather, it is easy for a kid who is poor or belongs to a lower middle class to become an IAS officer. The luxuries and comforts make the rich kid less prone to adapt to hard work.

There are hundreds of excuses for the failure of a loser, but for a winner, there is only one reason sufficient for his success. Hence, again, here it matters how you take your failure. You can create hundreds of excuses for hiding your weakness, or you can take a lesson and go ahead for chasing your success. Just assess yourself; if someone achieves something, then how do you feel by his or her achievement? The general reaction is that everyone feels jealous if he or she sees the achievement of others, except your parents. The jealousy is more acute when the relative is closer or living next door. Hence, as a normal person's reaction, it is a very common thing, but a better reaction is that such achievements shall inspire you to do better so that similar achievements shall also come your way. Here comes how you take things: the choice is yours.

During your childhood or as a student, you might have been scolded in your class by your teacher in front of all students. How did you feel after that insult? Did it inspire you to do better and mend your ways, or did you feel ashamed of it? It can work either way; you may have been encouraged to do better in your class, or you might have gone into depression and hidden your face from the class. The choice is yours in how you take such insults.

During our teenage, we have different types of groups of friends and company of friends. Some are full of intelligent persons, and some are of smokers, drinkers, or undisciplined guys. It depends on you in which group you wish to align with. Choice is yours.

I just want to say here again that the sequence matters. Here, you will have a comfortable life later if you work hard for the initial few years, or if you enjoy the comfortable life now, then you have to work hard your whole life. Choice is yours.

> **Enjoy Initially ——→ Work Hard Whole Life.**
>
> **Work Hard Initially ——→ Enjoy Whole Life.**

Glass Half-Filled Or Half-Empty.

We have heard a number of motivational stories about the glass half-filled or half empty. It is you or your nature which decides your vision. I have narrated a number of examples for you so that you can decide which one is better, and kindly choose that one, but the other options are also available to you. Choice is yours.

I am giving various cases of real life just to apprise you about two options you always have in life.

I came across such a situation when my father bought a TV for our family in 1989 when I was in 11th standard. Initially, my father was reluctant to buy the TV because he was sceptical that I would waste my time watching TV instead of studying for my

Engineering entrance examination. However, I convinced him that I wanted it so that I could watch UGC (University Grants Commission) programmes in the afternoon, which were very useful for my education and career. Eventually, the TV, as a new family member, arrived in our home. Surprisingly, I only watched UGC programmes for an hour, but my father started watching for 3 to 4 hours daily (all sorts of programmes like Alif Laila, Mahabharat, and Gul Gulshan Gulfam, etc.). This was jeopardising my Engineering entrance exam preparation. One afternoon, I disconnected the antenna wire and disrupted the TV connection. Finally, no UGC, no TV, no disturbance. Here, the choice was mine.

26

Have a Faith on God

"Coming together is a beginning. Keeping together is progress. Working together is success."

– Henry Ford

During our student life, we hardly have any time for worship and visiting religious places. However, we must have faith in our God and visit such places at least once a month. Every day, take at least 5 to 10 minutes to meditate and thank God for all that he has given you. During exam days or whenever you feel depressed, simply sit in front of your God for a few minutes, close your eyes, and concentrate. You will feel energised and refreshed.

I have given a formula for Success in other chapter of this book.

$$S = c(L \times I)$$

Where 'c' is the factor beyond our control, it is a variable constant ranging from 0 to 1. Here, the control of 'c' lies with God, depending on your stars and luck. Between the ages of 15 to 20 years, there is a slight sense of pride in almost every student due to their intelligence. They do not believe in things like God, destiny, luck, and stars. However, when they fail in exams or do not perform well, the role of God begins, and they start believing in God.

Initially, they think that their achievements are completely based on their talents and hard work, and there is no role of luck and God, hence sometimes arrogance creeps into their minds. So, I always recommend 5 minutes of meditation. I am saying that you should have faith in God so that you can put blame on God for your failure, and that will prevent you from falling into depression or being prone to suicidal tendencies.

Whenever you fall sick, at that time, faith in God will be very helpful, and you will feel a positive energy by listening to some religious songs like bhajans, etc. Always visit nearby temples, mosques, churches, gurdwaras, etc., based on your religious faith, nearly once a month, and sit there for 10 to 15 minutes, concentrating on God. You have to thank God after each and every achievement in your life.

Accept the things if the time is not in your favour or luck is against you. No need to get depressed. Keep on doing hard work, nothing else. Results will come for your hard work. There is a tradition in Hinduism that whenever we are going for any big task like exams or selections, then we have to touch the feet of our parents for taking the blessings of our parents or elders, it gives a positive energy into mind. If you are living away from your parents then just touch the feet of any statue, photo or idol of God.

27

English is a Medium Only

"A successful man is one who can lay a firm foundation with the bricks others have thrown at him."

– David Brinkley

In the 1980s, the ratio of Hindi medium students was much higher than it is today. This was because Hindi medium schools, which were predominantly affiliated with the State Education Board, were prevalent in small towns. English medium schools were mainly found in big cities across various States. In Hindi-speaking States like Madhya Pradesh, Uttar Pradesh, Rajasthan, and Bihar, even the English medium schools in small towns were in name only, as everything was taught in Hindi, with only examinations being conducted in English. Very few teachers were proficient in English; some taught in English while the rest used Hindi. However, the conditions have now changed significantly, with many well-trained teachers in English medium schools. Kendriya Vidyalaya is present in every district, providing education in English medium.

English hardly matters for maths, physics, and other science subjects because the concepts matter more than the language or medium. However, for humanities subjects like history and civics, the art of writing is crucial. Therefore, you need an artistic command over the language for humanities subjects. But during an Engineering or Medical degree, language or medium hardly matters.

During the 1980s, the success rate of Hindi medium (or vernacular language) students in IIT, Engineering Services, Civil Service exams, etc., was much higher than that of English medium school students. This was because these non-English medium students generally grew up with a slight inferiority complex when comparing themselves with English medium school students. English medium students had an upper hand in speaking fluent English to impress girls, boys, or class teachers, which resulted in them having many girls around them. This inferiority complex is more prevalent among Hindi medium students in villages. Even today in metros like Delhi or Mumbai, those who are fluent in English tend to look down on Hindi medium individuals. Due to this inferiority complex, Hindi medium students work hard to achieve something to reduce or eliminate that gap.

Initially, they think that without English there is no career or future, but I want to assure you that English is just a language like Hindi or other vernacular languages. It can be improved in a few months by hard work and study. The only problem will be in fluent speaking; it is either God-gifted or develops when your parents speak only in English at home. Otherwise, it is very difficult to learn, but at the same time, it is not impossible too. If you are determined, then it can also be improved in a certain long period.

You can just learn a lesson from Chinese guys. They have their own language in computers and software because they don't learn or speak English. Hence, they develop all software in their own language, and they love their language or mother tongue. They feel proud speaking in their language, while we feel an inferiority complex whilst speaking in Hindi and pride in speaking in English. Therefore, Hindi (or any vernacular language) and English, you should learn both. These two languages have their roles in India as well as in foreign countries.

Don't worry if you don't have a girlfriend or boyfriend because of this language issue, but once you get selected in IAS, IPS, or in any service, or become an engineer, doctor, or any successful professional, then only you will realise how much importance you were giving to a non-relevant thing like language.

28

Sequence Matters

"If you don't like the road you're walking, start paving another one."

– Dolly Parton

Although I have covered this "Sequence or the order matters issue" in the recharging of body and mind chapter, I am devoting a full chapter to it because it is very relevant for students appearing in competitive exams. The sequence or order matters in the life of every student. There are two ways of studying and playing games: you can follow either "study then play" or "play then study."

Generally, the normal students do the second one because they feel studying is a burden and an activity that needs effort. However, exceptional students do the reverse. They adopt the first strategy of reading first and then going for play. The first mechanism is better on multiple accounts. If we study first and then play, the duration of playing games will be used for recharging our mind. Hence, after playing, you can read again afresh with a fully recharged mind. But if you do the reverse - play first, then study later - you will feel enervated and will not be able to concentrate on your studies. Therefore, it is better to use the slot of playing games, watching TV, taking meals, or taking a nap, to recharge yourself in between the two study sessions.

The difference between studying and playing games is that studying requires effort and concentration, whereas playing games is effortless as far as the mind is concerned. In games, you can play anytime, but except for chess, all other games require prior physical fitness. In chess, you need more concentration similar to what is needed in studying. Studying requires a fresh mind, fully recharged after a good nap, sleep, or rest. If you play a game first, it becomes difficult to concentrate on studying, and you will feel tired. Mental tiredness is more relevant here than physical tiredness.

Hence, generally, it happens that kids want to play first and then want to study later. We have to reverse this sequence; they should study first and then go for playing games. For studying, you must be mentally as well as physically fully recharged and energised, but for playing games, you must have physical energy only.

29

Complex of Height and Complexion

"Never let success get to your head and never let failure get to your heart."

– Drake

There are various types of inferiority complexes in the minds of students, but these inferiority complexes can play a very positive role in the selection process for Engineering, Medical entrance, and ultimately in Civil Services such as IAS, IPS, etc. The chapter is very sensitive, and I don't want to hurt anybody based on gender, racism, culture, regionalism, or any other grounds.

Generally, students from villages or small towns often develop a bit of an inferiority complex. This could be due to feeling less smart compared to those from metropolitan cities, or it could be related to fluency in English. I am not generalising, but merely highlighting common trends in society. These students mainly come from Hindi medium schools in villages, especially in the North Indian States. Even today, there are hardly any English medium schools in remote areas or villages. Although the government has established Kendriya Vidyalaya in every district, in many villages, schools are non-existent, making English medium schools a distant dream for these communities.

Another complex is that of height. There are many students who are intelligent and hardworking but have below-average height. Because of this, they feel a little bit of shyness in their nature, and sometimes lack confidence.

Next, inferiority complex is about complexion or skin colour. It was prevalent in joint families in the 1980s. Society has changed significantly in the last 40 years, but it was widespread in the 1980s. Particularly in joint families, it served as a basis for comparison between two males or two females. If one had a fairer complexion than the other, it became a common topic of discussion in the absence of the person with darker skin. This comparison was the most dangerous within families, even among siblings with the same parents. Thankfully, society has evolved over the last 40 years, and this issue has taken a back seat.

Because of these four inferiority complexes in my engineering life and during my Delhi stay for Civil Services exams preparation, I lacked the confidence. Because of this, I did not have any girlfriend throughout my life, but sometimes I felt very jealous after seeing my colleagues with their girlfriends. My first girlfriend was my wife, Richa Khairha.

The inferiority complexes have their own positive role to play in the career formation of the students. Generally, those students who have such inferiority complexes have ample time for their studies. They don't have a girlfriend or boyfriend, allowing them to devote 100% of their time to their career or studies. They have nothing to distract their minds from these secondary things. They offset the shortcomings by fully devoting themselves to their studies. These complexes motivate them to do better and better in any field, whether in study, sports, arts, or music, etc.

When I joined my engineering college SGSITS, Indore, in 1990, I was full of these inferiority complexes. I was short in height, dark-skinned, and less smart compared to students from Indore, Bhopal, Bhilai, and Raipur. My English was pathetic, and even today, it's still the same. The reason was that I was reading English from the keys (or Kunji) just to pass the exam until 12th. My whole concentration was on Maths, Physics, and Chemistry, or you can say only the science subjects because I decided to do engineering when I was in 7th standard.

For Maths and Science subjects, English hardly matters. Due to this neglect of English over the last six years, I failed in the compulsory English paper in PET. Hindi medium students are very strong in grammatical English. They can also improve their writing skills in English with one year of hard work. However, improving fluency in English is a very, very difficult task.

In 1990, I decided to improve my writing skills in English. Hence, I started reading small news in the English newspaper "Free Press" published from Indore. After six months, I began reading the bigger news, and then I delved into the editorial section of the Free Press. After a year, I switched to the Times of India and purchased a good dictionary from Collins Cobuild, as suggested by Mr. Rajeev Jain, the elder brother of my room partner, Sanjeev Jain. Mr. Rajeev Jain was also a senior from the computer branch at my college. The dictionary was excellent in illustrating the usage of any word. I have kept that dictionary for over 31 years.

I want to request all the students, whether from Hindi medium or from English medium, not to neglect English as a subject or as a language. It is very much required if you are going abroad, appearing in interviews for Civil Services from an English medium, or pursuing your Medical or Engineering degree. Today, the percentage of English medium schools has increased compared to the 1980s. The whole world is a global village; one day or the other, you will have to go abroad for work or for further study. I would urge the students not to make the same mistake I did in my life by neglecting English.

In 1996 and 1997, both years, my scores in the written papers of the Civil Services examination were much higher than the scores of many IAS and IPS officers. However, due to the interview score, my rank was 251 and 218 respectively in those years.

In all Hindi medium students, there is background translation in their minds. They first think in Hindi, then try to translate that into English. Hence, in writing, it does not reflect, but during interviews or vivas, it reflects in their personalities.

In 1996, it was mandatory to appear only in English language for an interview if the optional papers were in English medium. However, if candidates were taking the written exam in Hindi medium, then they had the option to choose English as a language for the interview, in addition to Hindi. Lack of confidence and inferiority complex of weak English were the reasons that many Hindi medium students scored poor in Interview of Civil Services, If they appear in interview in English medium.

Here, I want to salute the guys and girls of Bihar. They are very simple, down-to-earth, and shy in nature. They silently prepare for Engineering and Medical entrance exams, and after that, for Civil Services examinations. They are never affected by the glory or shine of the whole world. Boyfriends or girlfriends are very secondary things for them until their selection. They never shy away from hard work or helping their parents with household chores and professional tasks in their business. After assisting their parents, they allocate a lot of time for their studies. They have two missions in mind: first is IIT, and the second is IAS. It is because of this, that the representation of students from Bihar is the highest in all competitive exams, including Civil Services.

I want to assure all the students that all these inferiority complexes vanish once you are selected in any competitive exam. These become secondary things once you get a job in the Civil Services or in any other field. Once you are selected, there will be many proposals awaiting marriage with you. So, keep away from these boyfriend-girlfriend relationships for the time being until you are studying. You can have a girlfriend or boyfriend only if she or he is a very good source of inspiration for you rather than a source of distraction.

30

Buy a Book and Borrow the Coat

"For the great doesn't happen through impulse alone and is a succession of little things that are brought together."

– Vincent Van Gogh

During the budgeting of our household expenses, we never keep or allot a dedicated fund for books or magazines. The only expenditures related to our children are for school fees, textbooks, or stationery, which are mandatory in any case. This same habit is passed on to our children as they grow up, and it continues from generation to generation. However, there are a few families who set aside some amount for books, newspapers, magazines, etc. Generally, such a habit is more common in families of teachers, professors, or those from West Bengal and from some South Indian States. Due to the absence of this practice, students often resort to borrowing books from friends to read, or some opt for photocopies of expensive books when only a few pages are needed.

Borrowing of the book is good if you are deciding whether to buy it or not, but if you are borrowing to read it and return it after noting down important things, then you are the poorest guy in the world, even though you have properties worth millions. You waste money every month on mobile recharge, some on smoking or drinking, etc., but we always try to save money when the issue comes up for investing in books. Even before investing in books, we think ten times whether the book will be useful for us or not, whether this money will go to waste, or if I already have a similar book, etc. Have you ever thought once, whenever you purchase a new T-shirt for yourself, even though you have more than ten T-shirts of the same colour and design?

Hence, always buy the book and borrow the coat instead of buying the coat and borrowing the book. Purchasing a new book has many advantages. First, it will improve your vocabulary, it will improve your reading habit, it will enhance your reading speed, and it will give you information. If you are reading a new book for an entrance examination, then you can get new tricks and ideas for solving numerical or some unique problems, or solutions you can find in it. Even during the preparation of Civil Services examination, you can find new topics in any book, which are sometimes directly asked in the exams.

An expenditure on any book will never go to waste. If you find that the book you purchased is not good or not useful for you, then just donate it to some needy person or give it to the library so 100 other people can read it. Generally, Indian parents or families give toys, clothes, or similar articles as gifts for birthdays to their children or other families. We never give a book or pen for such occasions because we presume that if the person already has the same book, then it would be a waste. Just remove this thinking from your mind. Even if there is a duplication of the book for the birthday boy or girl, then he or she can give it to a more needy person who doesn't have it. Don't we do it for Soan-papdi during Diwali? The same Soan-papdi passes through 6 to 7 hands before its expiry of 6 months till Holi, and finally, our household maid or driver consumes it at the end.

Why we think ten times before spending on a book. It is not just spending; it is an investment that will come back as a great fortune, but in due course. I never borrowed the book or the coat; I borrowed money to buy the book.

The first book, other than the textbooks, I purchased, was the English to Hindi dictionary by Prof R.C. Pathak (Bhargava's Dictionary) which I bought when I was in standard VIII. It cost me forty-five rupees. 40 rupees I won in gambling during one Diwali night, and Rs. 5, I borrowed from a family member. At that time, in 1985, it was the only dictionary available at that price in the small town. The dictionary was very useful for understanding English words.

I want to request all parents to gift one good book to your kids every year, so that he or she will study something different from the classroom study. It may be a general knowledge book, a book of quantitative numerical on mathematics, or a logical reasoning book so that an additional skill will develop in the kids.

There are many advantages of buying books in itself and buying a hard copy instead of a Kindle edition. If you borrow the book, read it, and return it, you can hardly retain 10% of the content. In a hurry, you might skip many chapters. Even if you make notes, you may still miss valuable information due to time constraints. However, if you buy the book, you can refer to it and read it anytime. By reading it repeatedly, you may discover very useful ideas or solutions within it.

In case of a reference book, I would suggest borrowing it so that you can xerox only a few pages if the book is very bulky. Secondly, you can borrow it if you are deciding whether to buy it or not.

What is talent...? After reading ten books, you can author the 11th. Hence, by reading books, you will create an author in you. Bibliophiles not only collect books or love them, but they also like the smell of a new book. The new pages of every book have a characteristic smell. In any bookstore, just go and smell the book; you will find it much better than many costly perfumes. After purchasing a book, always put the date, price, shop name, and city name on the second page of the book. After finishing it, put the date on the last page of the book and the time of finishing it. You will feel nostalgic if you see the same after 5 years or more. You will feel an attachment to the book after recalling the days when you first read it.

Books are the best friends if you have a good reading habit. After a monotonous life in any job, you will find a good companion in books; hence, in your free time, you can read them because every job can lead to a boring life after a certain age. Instead of fighting with your spouse, it is better to spend time with books. Books never argue. Whether you like the idea given in them or not, they will never retaliate.

Kindle edition of an eBook is good because you can keep multiple books in it, but you cannot mark relevant points, or highlight the lines as easily as you can in paperback books using multiple colours or a pen. The stress on your eyes is less with paperback books because you are reading by reflected light, unlike on a computer where the light comes from behind the page.

Always visit a bookshop or library every week, or at least every month, to read new books or purchase new books. Reading books keeps you alive. Similarly, you can do this with newspapers and monthly or fortnightly magazines. In whatever way you like, you have to keep your reading habit alive; never try to read the full book at the bookstall. It is a very sad part that some readers read the full book but purchase none from them, or they read the book at the bookstall and order from online platforms just to save a few rupees. Book sellers make a livelihood from these shops; they expect that you will buy something from them, so please don't break their expectation.

Always choose the books in the field of your interest and develop an expertise in that field. Try to write on that topic, albeit slowly. One day, you will find that you have a good collection of articles on that topic, and you will be in a position to write a good book.

31

Hostel Life and Team Spirit

"Some people want it to happen, some wish it would happen, others make it happen."

– Michael Jordan

It is generally seen that whenever students live in hostels or in areas developed as study centres like Jia Sarai, Ber Sarai, Mukherjee Nagar, Rajendra Nagar in Delhi, and coaching classes in Kota, their scores or performances are better than students who are living in isolation. In group study, you learn a lot of things, new tips, and tricks from other students, and you also share your own study strategies; hence, it is a win-win situation for all of you. Kota is developed as the biggest study centre for entrance exams in engineering and medical. Almost every year, the top students come from these coaching classes.

The main role in their achievement is played by the team spirit or hostel life. When these students live thousands of kilometres away from their homes, they act as parents for each other, helping and taking care of one another in case of illness, and also providing financial assistance in times of money shortage. They encourage each other because there is no room for jealousy among them; the competition is among 1 million students, not just a few. The students share secret tips with each other if they have a tendency to share, believing in comradeship and team spirit. The achievement or good score of one student encourages rather than discourages or depresses them. They never feel jealous; instead, they take it positively as motivation to improve themselves further. There is always a healthy competition and a positive atmosphere.

Hostel life is a good tool to reduce depression or to eliminate it completely, and an average student can seek guidance from an intelligent peer for problem-solving. Hostel life is the best period of your life; you should not miss it. Whether it is during graduation or entrance examination periods for medical or engineering, etc., it is a **"Not To Miss Opportunity."** It is beneficial for the mental development of students, instilling confidence for their whole lives and fostering comradeship and team spirit.

Part V

SOME MORE LESSONS

A. For Parents

32

Mild Counselling of Kids

"In order to be irreplaceable, one must always be different."

– Coco Chanel

In the era of the 1960s to the 1980s, there was a trend of family business. There was a shop, and every member of the joint family would sit in this shop in turn. I used to sit there after my school hours, on Sundays, or during holidays for the full day. It was where we learned how to do business and how to run a shop.

In the 1960s, the Indian economy was in a nascent stage and mainly dependent on agriculture and small businesses. The service sector had a very poor contribution to the country's economy. Even by the 1990s, the situation had hardly changed. However, the service sector flourished after the arrival of Windows 95, launched by Bill Gates. This led to a trend among students to pursue Computer and Information Technology. The brain drain began in the late 1990s, and the country's dependence on the service sector grew from 2000 onwards, leading to a decline in the agriculture sector. A similar trend was observed in micro-businesses. The reason behind this shift was the fragmentation of joint families into nuclear families after the 1980s. A single shop was no longer sufficient to sustain the entire family's expenses, so the shop was divided into two to four parts, depending on the number of brothers. Each part of the shop was then run by a different family member. Subsequently, their sons sought alternative means of income through education, such as pursuing engineering or medical studies. The new generations gravitated towards the service sector because the divided family businesses could no longer support their families adequately. These fragmented nuclear families began to migrate to metropolitan areas to enter the service sector, while some were attracted to the USA or other countries from 1995 onwards, thanks to the problem Y2K.

The joint family and the joint family businesses had their own benefits and limitations. The limitations were: the earnings were limited and had to be distributed among all. Additionally, even the inefficient members of the family had the same claim on profit as the efficient and hardworking members.

After a certain time, the business earnings were not sufficient to run the whole family because of the population explosion in India, in general, and in joint families in particular. The good thing was that we were not too emotional during the joint family era. Everything was open to each other. The same meal was taken by all the members of the family, with no place for pizza, burgers, or cold drinks because there was no surplus money with any member. Hence, we were eating only healthy food not by choice but by compulsion.

But in those 20 years of my life in a joint family, I have never heard of a single suicide case in my whole town. No one even knew the meaning of depression at that time. I came to understand the real meaning of depression after I joined the service. In 2021, I was posted in Kota when I heard about such depression in the lives of students who come to Kota to study in coaching for Engineering and Medical.

The root cause of such depression is the "Being Too Emotional Nature" of the student. Earlier, in a joint family, we used to share everything with our parents, uncles, and elder brothers, but today's siblings have hardly anyone to share their tension. Their parents are the only relatives living nearest to them, and no one else.

During the 1980s, we were slapped by anyone: father, uncle, brothers. My memory is very good; even then, I forgot how many times I have been slapped by these elders. But behind these slaps, there were some mistakes committed by me, and there were lessons in each slap for me that led my life to betterment. Similarly, every elder member scolded me for one reason or the other. But again, that scolding was responsible for improvement in my nature, study, or career.

Now come to today's kids. They are highly emotional. Slapping is just a thing in imagination. Rather, scolding by parents, even a little bit, hurts them so deeply that they feel insulted for many days. In the joint family, the scolding or slapping by an uncle was pacified by the father, or vice versa. But today, there is no one to pacify the kids if their father has fired or scolded them for any mistake. Here, mistakes are committed from both sides; hence rectification has to be done from both sides.

Firstly, parents have to understand that their kids are highly emotional and that there may not always be someone available to console them. Simultaneously, the children need to comprehend that parental guidance is provided for their benefit and future. Therefore, parents should strive to be good friends to their sons or daughters, adopting a friendly approach while maintaining a respectful distance to prevent the children from taking undue advantage. Occasional gentle counselling by parents is necessary, along with closely monitoring the progress and behaviour of the children in this emotionally charged era.

Now comes the role of alternatives: Today, most of the parents are in the service sector and they are living either in a metro or in a B town. Such parents hardly have anything to give their kids except a few lakhs of rupees as inheritance or a flat in some multi-storey building. But that is not sufficient for the livelihood of their kid.

In a joint family, there was a family business which stood next to us in case of our failure or as an alternative for giving us livelihood. This is missing in the lives of today's students. Hence, they think that if they fail in Engineering or Medical entrance, then there is no option left for them for their career. This type of anxiety leads them to depression and then finally to suicidal tendencies. Here comes the role of parents to be in touch with their kids, understand their psychology, and watch their performance if they are living away from their homes. Our upbringing is not done like the Chinese do; they are groomed by a mother tiger, and their kids are much stronger emotionally compared to Indian kids. We have to handle them differently.

My father, during my entire preparation for the IAS exam, used to tell me, "In case you fail the Civil Services exam, don't worry, you have a shop as another option. You are an engineer, so I am sure you will do better than I did in my life and you will further expand my business." These words from him gave me a lot of energy, stamina, and confidence for my studies, knowing that I had a plan B in place in case of failure in the Civil Service examination.

The Indian kids become too emotional because we have followed the Western culture in our home for the nuclear family. As we have followed the Western culture, our kids are more pampered, leading them to a very comfortable life. Consequently, even a small counselling session by parents can hurt them significantly. There should be a slight fear in the minds of kids, as well as respect for their parents, so that they will obey their parents and understand their parents' wishes. However, this should happen in a very friendly manner. The counselling or scolding by parents should be balanced so that the students do not fall into depression or develop suicidal tendencies. Simultaneously, they should not take liberties with their parents and should give due respect to them. Parents should bear in mind that they should counsel only occasionally and not make it a regular occurrence in dealing with their kids.

Because of Western culture, beating and scolding by teachers have been banned in Indian schools. Therefore, there is less fear today than there was in the 80s and 90s, but still, there is a little fear and respect in the minds of students towards their teachers. This fear gives the students' respect to the teachers, and they follow and obey their teachers more than their parents.

My father used to wake me up at 4 o'clock in the morning, although it was very irritating at that time initially, but later it became my habit to wake up at 4:00 a.m. I started studying some good topic for 3 to 4 hours. By the time of school, I was ready with all the subjects' revision, which helped me a lot in my whole career.

Strange but a reality that water supply was the main alarm for waking up all joint family members because the water supply started at 5 or 6 a.m. in the morning and lasted for 1 hour. So, everybody was ready with buckets or pitchers to fill during this one hour of water supply. That water supply helped me with my early rising and aided me in my career because it was possible only in the joint family.

33

Waste Versus Invest

"You learn more from failure than from success. Don't let it stop you. Failure builds character."

– Unknown

Every parent wants their kids to get selected in Engineering, Medical, or in whatever field they want to pursue. Hence, they are keen to invest a few lakhs of rupees so that their wards' future will be secured, and they will attend some prestigious college in the country or abroad. From day one, they anticipate a Rate of Return (ROR) on that investment. The rate of return comes in the form of selection in the entrance exam as a short-term capital gain and in the form of a handsome salary as a long-term capital gain, perpetually throughout their whole life.

When I was in Kota in 2021, I used to visit the coaching classes and hostel buildings. An average charge (Rs. 100000 per annum) for good coaching classes is not too much, but the expenses of the hostels are a major part, nearly Rs. 25,000 per month including meals, etc., which is nearly Rs. 3 lakhs per year, plus some other charges for stationery and daily expenses. Just assume it is also nearly Rs. 50,000 for a year; hence, roughly it is Rs. 450,000 per annum, including all expenses. Hence, if your ward is going for a 1-year course after taking a drop and completing the 12th class, then parents have to spend yearly Rs. 4.5 lakh in one year.

Parents generally spend that amount happily, assuming it is a lifetime expense with a good return for the career of their kids. Here starts the whole economics and its calculation of Rate of Returns. This ROR is very dangerous for the life of kids. The ROR for any big project is a good thing, and you calculate beforehand to decide whether to go ahead with this project or not. Generally, if it is more than 14%, then it is good enough; otherwise, to drop the project. It is a very common practice in the corporate world and in the government sector so that investors or companies can recover the cost in nearly 7-8 years. Then, after that, the whole setup will run free of cost, as far as capital cost is concerned, for the rest of the balance life of the capital asset.

But this strategy fails in the human resource development of our kids. Once the parents send their kids away from home for these coaching classes, they feel that they have invested in a good project where ROR is enormous and without any loss. These parents have to understand the difference between the project investment and human resource investment for their kids. The project never fails; it will either give you exceptional or expected results, or give you less than expected returns, but it never fails completely. Even in case of all adversity, if it fails completely, then also you have some residual value or depreciated value to recover your cost, but for the education of your kids, you have to think differently.

First, the parents have to stop thinking that it is an investment for which they are waiting for a good rate of return; rather, it is a duty of theirs, and they have to spend that money on the upbringing of their child.

Second, from day one they have to think differently that they have wasted their money in the education of the child, for which the rate of return is nil. Then only they will sit peacefully for the rest of the period of struggle of their kids. It is like a lottery betting, but here the chances of winning are very high, 50%, as compared to conventional lottery.

Just assume that you have donated that money to charity rather than invested it in your kid. Hence, even if your kid fails in these exams, you will not feel bad because you have already donated that money to charity for a good cause.

I humbly request all parents that any money you spend on the human resource development or education of your child will never go to waste. Chances are there that you will get the return immediately, or if not immediately, then after a little lag. You will see that the returns are manifold than your expectations, but just wait; it takes time if not immediate.

Thirdly, parents have to be in regular touch with their kids and understand in which direction their kids are thinking or going, without disturbing them in their day-to-day study, if they are living away from them in a hostel or otherwise.

It is the duty of the parents to console the kids, that whatever they are spending on their kids, the kids should never worry or bother about that. The parents also have some plan B for them in case of being unsuccessful in desired exams. Parents have to visit the kids in the hostel as per their comfort, monthly or quarterly, and motivate them for study, relax them, and tell them plan B in a lighter way.

Therefore, parents have to think differently by treating that amount, as spent on charity or donation or even assume that it is just a waste and they should not wait for quick returns. It is investment on human resource or education, the return may come immediately or it may come later but it will definitely come.

> **Parents think like this:**
>
> Investment ⟶ Waiting For Returns ⟶ Unsuccessful Results ⟶ Feeling Like A Waste.
>
> **Parents should think like this:**
>
> Charity Or Donation Or Waste On A Horse Riding ⟶ Donated Hence No Expectation Of Returns ⟶ If Unsuccessful, There Is No Additional Loss. / If Successful, The Rate Of Return Is Infinite.

In case of the second option, whatever comes with success will be a bonus to your donated money as a return. It will give you enormous happiness because it is an infinite gain on your already donated money.

Hence, to summarise, expenditure on human resources cannot be compared one to one with the expenditure in a corporate project. So, parents have to think differently about their expenses and have a plan B ready for their kids in case they are unsuccessful in achieving their desired goal.

Kids are always in a tender age in their 9th to 12th class, hence they are also very emotional. They are very touchy about statements such as those generally given by parents: "We have wasted so much money on you. We expected that one day you would become an engineer or doctor. Have you heard that Mr. XYZ's son has topped the entrance exam for Engineering or Medical? Do you realise how hard it is to earn money? Money does not grow on trees, etc."

If parents feel that they are not able to afford the expenses of their kids, then they should not send them for coaching. If they feel that their money is more precious than the lives of their kids, then they should not send them for such courses. In such cases it is better parents don't spend anything on their wards for such courses at least, it will save the lives of their kids.

"Small returns without expectation" gives much more happiness than "Big returns with expectations."

B. For Students

34

Coaching Centres: Necessary Evils

"True winners are those who relentlessly climb the ladder of success while the world rests in slumber. The path to victory is illuminated by the resilience of those who dare to ascend when others choose to sleep."

There are a number of coaching centres in Kota for Engineering and Medical entrance examinations, and similarly in Delhi for Civil Services examinations. The purpose of these coaching centres is to provide you with a healthy competitive atmosphere, and in case of any doubt, you can seek help in solving problems from the experts of each subject. You can expect a maximum five percentile improvement in your scores in JEE, or a similar improvement in other exams, but coaching classes cannot raise your score from 60 to 99 percentile. This is because of the over expectations that can make you feel depressed initially when joining the coaching.

The coaching centres always try to segregate the students based on their intelligence into various batches so that anyone will be kept in a section or class of one's intelligence level. Just imagine you are an average aptitude guy and you are kept in the star batch of topper students. Then, within a month, you will leave the coaching and go back to your home because the speed of the super intelligent students is very high in understanding and in solving the problems. You may not be able to sustain this pressure.

I am giving you some tips for maximising the benefits from these coaching centres. These tips may be quite helpful once you join these classes.

Firstly, have a good foundation of basic study. Generally, students start joining coaching classes without any knowledge base of that class. In JEE or NEET, once they pass the 10th standard, they end up in these classes immediately without studying a single chapter of the next class. Hence, it is better to finish the syllabus of the next class for relevant subjects. If you are not able to finish that, then at least finish two or three chapters of each subject before going to the coaching classes. Always stay ahead of the coaching class's study.

Generally, in all good coaching classes, the tutors of each subject will tell you what they will teach you in the next lecture. Hence, always read that chapter a day before and note down the pages, paragraph, or problem where you have some doubt or you are not able to understand. It has three benefits. First, you will be familiar with the subject or topic being taught in the class. Second, your doubts will be clarified in the classes, and third, it will be a revision for you because you have already read it a day before.

Don't expect too much from these classes. I am repeating it again that coaching centres are providing you a platform for healthy competition and for clearing doubt or for some guidance.

Don't expect that they will do a miracle in your life, as they have their own limitations. There are limited seats in every examination, and each one cannot get selected. They can guide you on how to score better or how fast and accurate you can solve a numerical. These coaching centres also encourage you to perform better, and they also counsel you whenever you feel depressed and discouraged. They also motivate you after telling you the names of the achievers who passed out from their classes previously.

It is better to join such coaching after 12th class, if you are an average or below average guy. But if you are an above-average or outstanding student, then it is better to join the coaching from 9th or from 11th because you have the capability to handle the speed in coaching classes for study. If you are a student of below-average aptitude, then it's better to complete the 12th first and appear in the entrance exam of Medical or Engineering as a first attempt before joining the coaching classes as a drop year. The average life expectancy is 65 years or above in India for a well-to-do family. Just imagine, if you lose one year from your life, then it hardly matters. Hence, joining coaching after 12th is better in two senses. First, you are well-prepared with the whole syllabus up to 12th standard before joining classes, and you have a strong base to understand new things and for better revision.

Secondly, by slow or normal speed of study in the school classes in 11th and 12th, you can understand everything and enjoy the student life in the school rather than in coaching classes. The dummy school culture has snatched the childhood of students. Hence you will be able to enjoy your school days in schools rather than in coaching classes. Generally, it is seen that the average or below average students go into depression, once they are not able to cope up the pressure of the coaching class's study. So, to sum up, it is a better strategy for them to complete the study of 12th and then join the coaching classes. **It is always better to lose one year of your life than to lose the life.**

Remember, the coaching centre is like a Motichur laddu of marriage. If you don't join it, you will miss something; if you join it, you will feel your most of the time is going in it. But the coaching is very much required in this time; otherwise, you will feel lagging behind the other students.

I want to give my own example here. I never joined any coaching classes until my completion of graduation. I joined the coaching classes in 1995 when I got selected in the Prelims of the Civil Services examination of 1995. From July 1995, I started attending Meridian classes at Ber Sarai in New Delhi. I paid the fees for all three subjects: Maths, Physics, and General Study. The head of the coaching, Shri Ashok Singh, then called me and asked whether I would be able to take all these classes of nearly 7 hours in a single stretch. I told him, "Sir, I just want to fail in this attempt with good marks so that I will be saved from attending coaching classes next year."

My purpose was not to get through that year because I was aware of my level of preparedness. But I was sure of cracking it the following year. Hence, I attended the classes for nearly 3 months without missing a single class. I was not aiming to understand everything; rather, my purpose was to learn tricks or tips for solving problems. I grasped how to solve the Simplex problem in Operations Research (OR) in mathematics and some other problems in ODE (Ordinary Differential Equation) and

PDE (Partial Differential Equation). Similarly, in Physics and General Study, I learned a number of tips and tricks for solving problems and answering concisely.

I failed in that Civil Services Mains examination of 1995, but I scored well in the optionals (Physics and Maths), GS papers, and in the essay as well. That encouraged me to appear the next year with full energy and vigour. The following year, I got selected in the Civil Service examination of 1996 and secured the 251st All India rank. My score was 436 out of 600 in mathematics (first paper 212 out of 300 and 2nd paper 224 out of 300). The tips from Meridian classes were very useful for maths. In the Physics first paper, my score was 180 out of 300 and in the essay 105 out of 200. It was okay for a Hindi medium student who appeared in the English medium in the Civil Service examination and was from an engineering background.

Here, the coaching helped me a lot, not for solving or explaining the whole syllabus for each and every question, but for guiding me and giving me some tips and tricks for solving questions. Again, the next year, in the 1997 Civil Service examination, I secured the 218th rank. Both times, I got into the railway.

The coaching done from July to October 1995 was very useful for my career and future. It guided me on how to reply in exams and how to frame my answers. No doubt, Meridian classes contributed a lot to my career. They gave me confidence for appearing in the Civil Services examination, which enabled me to score better in mathematics in both attempts. My mathematics score was much higher than the scores of many IIT graduates.

Hence, the role of coaching is 20%, and 80% is your own study and hard work. It is this 20% that matters at the end, which is contributed by coaching classes. But before that, you must achieve 80% by your own efforts. However, the average students think differently; they believe that it is an 80% contribution by the coaching and 20% their efforts of self-study.

Hence, it is a synergy of your self-study and guidance from coaching classes. Therefore, overdependence on coaching classes will be detrimental to your study. Give priority to your self-study and use these coaching classes as a supporting tool to score even better.

Generally, it is seen that students who join coaching start studying many reference books instead of reading a good book completely. It is better to complete the best book for each subject and then go for the reference book, but students generally do the reverse. If you complete a book thoroughly for each subject, you will be able to solve many problems. In case of an exceptional problem, you can refer to reference book for any topic that is explained better in that reference book. Also, the kids are entangled with all types of study material; hardly having time for revision. Therefore, it is better to revise the best book repeatedly instead of reading multiple reference books.

Coaching is good if it is for the revision of all topics, you have studied earlier. **It is good** if you are seeking clarification on a few problems instead of understanding the whole syllabus. **It is good** if you are going ahead of the coaching classes' syllabus. **It is good** if your study hours are much more than what you need for coaching, and you have enough time for self-study as well.

35

Interviews of the Achievers Like IAS, IPS Officers etc

"Optimism is the faith that leads to achievement. Nothing can be done without hope and confidence."

– Helen Keller

Students are full-time busy with entrance examinations for Engineering, Medical, Law, etc. Hence, they hardly have time to read magazines or newspapers, but they must read interviews of the top IAS achievers and some special achievers. These interviews or news pieces are very motivational and inspiring; such achievers provide good guidance, techniques, and tricks for better study to crack competitive exams.

In Hindi newspaper, I used to read the success stories (fame called SUYAS in Hindi) of XYZ student or the topper of the Board examinations. It inspired me personally to appear in Engineering entrance exams and Civil Services examination. Reading motivational stories of successful individuals or achievers can have a strong inspiring force to motivate you. Reading the success stories of achievers will help you choose your career in a specific field.

Every year, the results are declared for the selected candidates in, Engineering, Medical, Law entrance examination and Civil Services examination. The print media in newspapers or magazines publish the interviews of the successful candidates. I suggest the students in class 8th, 9th, or even senior students to read these interviews and learn how these successful candidates study in their life for achieving their success. You adopt the best of their methods, which should suit you.

It is much better if you have a chance to meet such achievers and take guidance from them. It will inspire more than reading their interviews in magazines. They will suggest you the reading strategy, some good books, and how to achieve success in your careers. If it is not possible, then watch the TV programme in which such successful toppers give interviews. These are also available on the YouTube channels of the successful candidates.

Another source of inspiration is the visit of the offices of IAS, IPS, Income Tax officers, IFS, District Judges or CEO of a big company, etc. If you have a chance of meeting them, well and good. If even you are not able to meet them, just observe the paraphernalia of these officers around their office. Just see their official vehicle, staff attached to them as an attendant, guard, or gunman, and their subordinate staff and officers, and the public who are there for their work from these officers. You can have a look at their residence also, from outside. Their huge mansion-style bungalow will work as a source of inspiration. For many officers, there may be a gunman or guard standing at the gate. After seeing all these, you will be inspired to work hard if you are really serious about achieving these successes in your life.

If you are in class 9th or 10th, try to visit top colleges in fields such as Engineering, Medical, Law, etc., and explore the campus and hostel areas. Seeing the students studying there may inspire you to take the entrance exam for your preferred field and give your 100%.

36

Immediate Failure Versus Final Failure

"I have not failed. I've just found 10,000 ways that won't work."

– Thomas Edison

Immediate failures are your short-term unsuccessful results of some less important events. They can be your poor results in an exam, failing in the first attempt, or failure in your day-to-day life, but these are not your final failures in life. These are rather small and necessary things to lead you to the final success. These failures are required very much at one time or the other in your life.

The students at a very tender age with immature minds are not able to understand the difference between immediate failure and final failure. Such students take immediate failure as a stumbling block in their career. These failures are the stepping stones for life and career instead of stumbling blocks. Every immediate failure, you have to take positively; you have to learn a lesson from these failures. Every time, you have to think about the shortcomings or mistakes committed in your efforts. You have to think about how to improve yourself or prepare yourself for the next attempt. You have to change your strategy next time and give your 100%, which was missed in your previous attempt.

Students can take these immediate failures in two ways. Either they can get depressed and adopt the wrong path, or they can use these failures as encouraging tools to motivate themselves and try to improve, getting themselves ready to face the new challenges.

Here, I want to share some of the immediate failures of my life. Each failure, I took positively, and I never felt humiliated by any failure in my life. Instead, I always tried to improve myself to face further challenges.

First failure of my life was in 1986 in the second stage of Science Quiz conducted by some Jabalpur Academy, which was searching for talent among science students in 9th and 10th standard. Again, the next year in 1987, I failed in the level 2 (second stage) of the same exam. In the same year, I failed in the NTSE exam also, which was conducted by NCERT.

In 1990, I failed in English paper of PET (Pre-Engineering Test), which was mandatory and qualifying for getting admission in REC (now called it NIT (National Institute of Technology)). The reason was very simple that I was from Hindi medium and there was no English Medium School in Panna so there was always a shortage of good English teachers. Because of failing in English, I could not get any REC college and I landed up in SGSITS Indore.

That was also equally good college like MACT and other REC colleges. There in hostel life of Indore, I tried to improve my English by reading newspaper and magazine of English. Since I decided to choose Maths and Physics as my optionals for Civil Services exams, then I did my Engineering in Electronics and Telecommunication just as a basic degree required for all

UPSC exams. Here in SGSITS, again I failed in each and every placement conducted by various companies in final year of Engineering.

Then came the final mission of my life: Civil Services examination of 1995. In this year, I qualified my prelims in my first attempt, but again I failed in the Mains exam. However, my score was very good in Physics, Maths, and Essay, which encouraged me to appear again with full preparation the next year.

Finally, I got the 251st rank in the 1996 CSE. It was the first job of my life in the Railway in RBSS. It was May 1997 when the final result of the Civil Services examination-1996 was declared. This time, I partially failed because I could not get the service of my choice, but I had a secured government job, so I was feeling relaxed.

We'll just go back three months in my life to 1997; that was the scariest part of my life, one I would never forget.

During our stay at Jia Sarai in New Delhi for preparation of the Civil Services examination, we used to call our parents every Sunday evening after dinner to inform amma (mother) and papa about our well-being. At that time, a mobile phone was a luxury in 1997, so we used to go to a nearby PCO. Since the time was fixed, my parents were always sitting near the phone at 9:05 p.m. because the call charges became one fourth of the usual full charge during the day. Hence, just to save money, we called after 9:00 p.m.

Generally, my parents picked up the phone in the third or fourth ring, but on that day, it was more than fifteen rings when my amma picked up the phone. I asked, "Where is papa?" because papa usually answered the phone first and then handed it over to amma. Before she could reply, I heard a metallic sound through the receiver. The sound resembled hollow pipes knocking against something on the floor. She then informed me that papa had been in an accident while riding his Luna. A rickshaw wala had collided with his Luna, breaking his leg.

A plaster was tied to his one leg by Dr. Jamdar of Jabalpur, and he was using the Walker (Baisakhi or walking sticks). The shop was closed for many days, and my papa told my amma not to tell me; otherwise, my study would be disturbed, and I would not be able to concentrate on my study. Since the shop was closed for so many days, so my family was running short of funds.

The next day I reached Panna. I found my papa was sleeping in the front-hall and the Walkers were inclined on his bed, with a Thali on the stool having some water in it, because he might have washed his hands in that after finishing his dinner. I was completely shattered at that time. I was so selfish that instead of thinking about his pain, leg and his health I was thinking about my study and about my next attempt and what, if I fail in Civil Services examination-1996. I was in a stage of complete shock of my life. It appeared to me as the final failure of my life, and I was just completely broken.

I was just thinking about that rickshaw wala and cursing him, who spoiled my whole life's hard work of 12 years in a fraction of a second. Many businessmen or you can say shopkeepers, and the neighbours were coming to see my father, and everybody was consoling me that "Your father is not able to walk, and he would be bedridden for a long time or might not walk in the near future. Then please wind up your study and come back to Panna and run your shop; otherwise, who will feed your family?" Some said, "You need a livelihood for your daily expenses of your life." Such suggestions were given by every alternate person who was visiting my home and meeting my father, but no one supported me either financially or morally to go ahead with my study.

All my dreams shattered; my whole ambitions had gone to waste. My whole 12 years of study appeared to me as going in a dustbin. I was very depressed on that day. It was 9:00 p.m. after my dinner, I was walking on the rooftop of my single-floor home. I was just watching the stars, the moon, and the Ram mandir (temple) behind my house. I was asking God, "why me?" that too at the most sensitive time of my life, after the second attempt of Civil Services Mains examination of 1996. The Mains exam was conducted just 4 months back in October to November 1996. During the cursing of 30 minutes to God and that Rikshaw wala, I decided to wind up my study and pack up all my study materials from Jia Sarai to come back to Panna to run the shop and take care of my papa. At 10:00 p.m., I called my Jijaji to get my reservation done at Jabalpur from Jhansi to Delhi in any train after 2 days.

The very next day, I also got the reservation done for returning back from Delhi to Satna (As there was no railway lines at Panna), finally to wind up my whole study of IAS exam. I have to take the train from Jhansi to Delhi the next day, but the day before that journey to Delhi, at around 3:40 p.m., my DoT phone rang. I picked up the call; on the other side, it was Manish Malviya (IOFS officer now), who was my engineering batchmate of SGSITS, Indore. Manish just asked me how I was and about my father as he was aware of my plan of returning back to Panna. He told me that there is no need to go back to Panna permanently because I have got selected in Civil Services Mains examination. So, he told me come to Delhi immediately and prepare for the interview. Since I was very tensed, I could not believe that. Then I confirmed it with Harish Ahuja, who also got selected in the Mains exam. That was the biggest turning point in my life.

Next day, I took the train and reached Delhi. Instead of going to Jia Sarai, I went to UPSC Shahjahan Road from New Delhi station. However, it was 10.00 pm at night, so I requested the guard to kindly open the gate because I had been selected in the written exams and I wanted to see my roll number in the list of nearly thirty A4 size papers. He noticed my hold-all luggage and water bottle in my hand, then he allowed me for 5 minutes. After finding my roll number, I felt relaxed and thanked the guard before returning to Hauz Khas. By walking, I reached Jia Sarai. Many Civil Service aspirants had gathered near Lucky Restaurant, where I discovered that the lists of selected candidates in Mains were displayed on the brick wall. I chuckled at myself, wondering why I had gone to UPSC to have the gate opened to see my results. However, there was a lot of enthusiasm about the selection, so those 30 minutes and the extra five rupees on the bus hardly mattered that day.

Mr Harish Ahuja, Mr R.K. Singh (we called him Dada; now he is Principal Secretary in MP Govt (IAS)) and I decided to join Bajiram and Rao classes for the preparation of the interview. Now, a financial crunch came; my father was almost bedridden, and the shop was closed for many days. I felt shy to ask my papa for the fees of Bajiram and Rao. Coincidentally, Ramji Tripathi, who was my good friend from childhood, senior to me, and working as a Junior Engineer in Doordarshan, was passing through Delhi station. He was posted in Sri Ganganagar, Rajasthan at that time, and during his journey to Panna, he had to take the train from Nizamuddin station.

He called me to come to the station, so I went to meet him and shared the complete condition of my family and the Civil Services examination interview. I told him, "Ramji, I don't have any money to join the interview's mock classes. It requires nearly 2000 rupees for fees and 500 rupees for conveyance by auto for 5 days." Ramji then offered his support with 2500 rupees. I assured him that I would repay him from my first salary if I got selected that year. Otherwise, I would return it when my papa resumed working at the shop. He reassured me, saying, "Don't worry, there is no hurry; just appear in the interview with full preparation."

I joined Bajiram and Rao classes with Harish and R.K. Dada. After all the interviews conducted by UPSC, the result was declared, and I got 251st rank, and I got the job. I returned the money to Ramji Tripathi with thanks, although not from the first salary but quite late, as there were many loans due on me. Today, Ramji Tripathi is not there in this world, but his memories and help during my worst days will be there forever in my mind for my whole life.

Just imagine, that would have been almost a complete or final failure for me, had I not been selected in the Mains of Civil Services examination of 1996. You know, if I had failed in the

Civil Services exam of 1996, then also, I would not have taken it as a final failure; rather, I would have tried for MPPSC exams from Panna.

My purpose in sharing my real-life example was simply to show that everyone faces challenges or problems in life. Don't give up; one day, you will achieve success in your desired goal or in any other target.

Here, I am giving various exams where I failed in the last 30 years.

- As I told you, in 1986 and 1987, in both years, I failed in the Science Quiz second stage.
- I failed in 1987 in the National Talent Search Examination conducted by NCERT.
- I failed in the Maths Olympiad in 1989.
- I failed in the English paper of the Pre-Engineering Test in 1990.
- I failed in Indian Air Force test conducted at Varanasi in 1993.
- I failed in Civil Services Mains examination of 1995
- I failed in GATE 1994 for admission to M.Tech.
- I failed in JNU's M.Phil entrance exam in 1994 for Physics.
- I could not get selected in any of the placements at my engineering college in 1993-94 during my final year.
- In 1995 and 1996, I failed in the Indian Forest Services examination when I appeared with optionals Physics and Maths.
- I could not qualify for the 1995 and 1996 MP Public Service Commission exams for Prelims.

- In 2008, I failed in the CAT exam for an MBA or PG diploma at IIMs.
- I could not do the post graduate programme in public management and policy (PGP-PMP) even after my selection in IIM Ahmedabad in 2009.
- I could not get selected in any deputation of various Ministries during my service.
- I performed very poorly in the GMAT and could not get admission to any college for an executive MBA.
- I was not empanelled into Joint Secretary Empanelment in 2020. It is a prerequisite for serving as Joint Secretary in Central government's ministries because of that I inspired to write this book as I was having a lot of free time to devote for writing my motivational book.

I just gave the details of all these exams where I failed, but in every failure, the score was not that bad. Every time, I was motivated to perform better. Always, the failures lead you to the final success. So, don't be afraid of these failures; they are there in everybody's life. In the life of every successful person, for bigger success, there are much bigger failures in their life. Hence, I request all hardworking students of Kota that failures are parts of your life; you can take these failures positively.

These are not your final failures. Just take these failures as motivational sources for your further study. The age of final failure is not 15 to 20. The only mistake committed by you is that you are taking immediate failure as your final failure. Recently, cases of suicide have been found in the age group of 15 to 20, but not after 23 years of age, because the age group of 15 to 20 students is very sensitive, and their minds are not able to understand the difference between immediate failure and complete failure. They think that Engineering and Medical are the only fields for a career, and that too from the best colleges only. While graduates, those who are preparing for Civil Service examinations or Public Service examinations, are mature enough to understand the meaning of immediate failure and final failure. Hence, these individuals never commit suicide. Hardly any case is heard in the age group above 23.

There are far fewer cases of suicide in Civil Service examinations compared to JEE or NEET examinations. This is because graduates have a degree in hand, are more mature, and understand their parents' concerns. The parents of these graduates are much older, so the Civil Services aspirants understand better that who will take care of their parents in case if they take such a drastic step of committing suicide.. With a degree for livelihood, their lives are more secure than those of Engineering or Medical aspirants. There is a 10-year age difference between the parents of a 15-year-old student and those of a 25-year-old graduate. The younger generations cannot comprehend their parents' situation in their absence, but a graduate can understand this better, preventing them from taking such drastic steps. Graduates realise their parents' future dependency on them.

I have dedicated a full chapter to those of my friends who are complete failures in study but not in their life. They are doing much better than many of us in life. They are final failures in study but finally successful in their lives.

37

Millionaires Losers

"Don't worry about failure; you only have to be right once."

– Drew Houston

This chapter is dedicated to those friends of mine who were failures in their studies but have succeeded in life. Today, they are better placed than me. I am referring to my four friends from Panna. Three of them could not get selected in the PMT even after preparing for the exam at various coaching classes. However, today they are millionaires running successful businesses and are among the top businessmen in Panna. One of them has a large showroom selling fridges, TVs, washing machines, etc., and holds an agency for an automobile company.

Another friend runs the largest shop selling clothes and dresses in Panna, earning millions every year. The third friend operates a school in Panna, which is one of the best in the area. This friend was with me at Jia Sarai preparing for the Civil Services exam. The fourth and last friend is an engineer turned reputable contractor, managing major government contracts. Additionally, he is actively involved in social services and politics. I am confident that one day he will become a cabinet minister in the Madhya Pradesh Legislative Assembly.

I am just giving the above examples of my friends so that you can understand that those were the immediate failures in their lives, but they were not failed completely. You can say that a few were failed completely in study but were not complete failures in life. The immediate failure in life or the complete failure in study, they have taken positively, and they have performed well in their plan B.

Another failure I want to quote is for the Civil Services exams. Those who failed in the Civil Service examination but could get good jobs in the State's Public Services examination (PSC) as SDM or Deputy SP, etc., or in other government jobs, are now also doing well.

The others who are complete failures in getting any government job, are running reputed coaching classes for IAS or PSC. They are also earning in crores, even though they failed in these exams. But today, they are making IAS, IPS, SDM, Deputy SP, etc., from their coaching classes. Some of them have opened various branches of their coaching classes in Delhi, Patna, and Allahabad. They never regret their immediate failures in their lives. Because of these failures, they are millionaires today.

So, you can see that Biggers are the successes, as Biggers were the failures. Similarly, those candidates who failed in the Engineering or Medical entrance exams, or those who could not get the top colleges, are running the top reputed coaching classes for Engineering and Medical entrance, and every year they are making hundreds of engineers and doctors who passed out from the top Engineering or Medical colleges after attending these coaching classes.

Remember one thing in mind that always dare to take the risk in your career and keep the plan B ready in case of any failure. If you follow this in your life, then you will never feel depressed, and no negative thoughts will come to your mind. Always keep in mind that if you could not achieve the best desired goal in your life as you planned earlier, then the other secondary options are not as bad or inferior as you think. For Medical, if not AIIMS, then other colleges of NEET or, if not NEET, then some other secondary colleges in small towns. Similarly, for Engineering, if not IIT, then some NIT or if not NIT, then some other engineering colleges. Likewise, for the branches also, if not computer, then Electronics or Mechanical, etc. In Civil Services also, if not IAS, then IPS, IFS, etc., or any other Group A or Group B services; another option is SDM or Deputy SP through the State Services or any other government jobs. If you could not secure that too, then there are very good private companies offering good jobs which are equally good.

You can just read the history of the world's top billionaires; then, you will find that they were big failures in their lives, but they never gave up. Rather, they were motivated by their failures, and finally, success came to them.

These small failures of your life are tests by God that make you stronger; hence, never be scared of these failures rather take them positively. God is keeping something bigger for you, just wait for the good time. Everything is destined to happen, but at a particular specific time, so just make effort, effort, and effort. Success will come automatically one day or the other.

38

How to Handle Various Pressures

"You've got to get up every morning with determination if you're going to go to bed with satisfaction."

– George Lorimer

The students are undergoing various pressures during their entrance test preparation.

First is the pressure of study in the coaching classes. There are a number of books and daily notes given by the coaching classes to study. The speed of teaching in coaching is much more than the speed of teaching in schools; hence, students have to enhance their study hours in daily routines. Apart from the daily coaching notes, there are reference books which they also have to go through for selected chapters and problems. This pressure is an inevitable part of the life of the students. This, they cannot eliminate from their daily life.

Second is the peer pressure. Every student cannot have the same aptitude attending the same coaching class; there is always a difference in the intelligence level of different batches in the coaching class, plus within the same batch, there is an aptitude difference. The students are always under tremendous pressure whenever their colleagues perform better and they cannot. If someone gets through the exam, then they feel a lot of pressure to achieve the same or better next year. Such types of peer pressure are visible during the tests conducted fortnightly by the coaching class. This pressure can be eliminated from the minds of the students. They have to compete with themselves to avoid such undue pressure; it will relax them in the test and in the final examination.

Third is the aspiring for the best college and the best branch, without compromising on that. Whenever any student of Engineering or Medical entrance joins the coaching classes, their expectation is to get into the best college and the best branch, like IIT Mumbai in computer science for engineering students, AIIMS for medical students, or NLU Bangalore for law students. Initially, they don't want to compromise on that, but as time passes, they realise their actual ranking. Hence, they have to have a plan B ready. They need to think about what comes next if the best is not achieved. They have to set targets based on their aptitude or talent rather than setting unrealistic goals. Unrealistic goals that are unachievable will lead them to depression.

Fourth one is society's and relatives' pressure. It is the most dangerous among all pressures, and it is very difficult to handle too. The only solution is to just ignore it rather than taking it to heart. When you go home, everyone starts asking what happened to your results, what your score was, the son or daughter of Mr. XYZ has got this rank or that rank in this exam or that exam. Such comments from neighbours or relatives feel like bombarding the minds of emotional individuals. There are two ways to handle such pressure: first and the best is to ignore it and avoid meeting such individuals, and the second one is to develop a thick skin and politely tell them, "Mind your own business, uncle or aunt."

Fifth is the sibling pressure, this pressure is basically internal to the mind of a student because of elders or younger siblings. It is generally seen that if an elder member is performing outstandingly in academics in the family, then the student comes under heavy mental pressure to achieve better or at least to that level. Similarly, if your younger one is outstanding, then you study under pressure to do better than him; otherwise, what will the parents think? Don't compare with anyone else; even in Mahabharat, the Pandavas were five brothers, each having a different talent incomparable with one another.

Sixth is parental pressure. It is very common in society that every parent expects that their kids perform well in any entrance exam for Medical, Engineering, or otherwise. Hence, to fulfil these expectations of parents, the kids start studying in that direction even though sometimes they may not be keen to go into that line of Medical or Engineering, etc. Parents imitate such things by seeing the achievements of the kids of other relatives or neighbours.

Actually, the decisive factor for the study of kids must not be the above pressure; rather, their own choice and aptitude shall decide in which field they want to go. Parents have to ask in which field their kids want to go and where they will be comfortable and excel, rather than forcing them to go into the field of the parents' choice. **The life of the kid is more precious than a future in a specific line.**

39

Interval of Depression

"More is lost by indecision than by wrong decision."

– Marcus Tullius Cicero

During continuous study, sometimes you will find that you are very bored. If you are unable to solve a problem or score poorly in a test, you will feel highly depressed. Here, just do one thing: immediately stop studying that topic and take a break for a few minutes or watch a movie or some relaxing TV serial. During this interval of depression, read something that you generally never used to read – exceptional and non-relevant things, but related to your study. Whatever you do in this most idle time, you will find one day that it was very useful for your exams or career.

Generally, whenever you find your study interesting, you keep on studying routine things. But whenever you utilise this idle time in depression, you will find that you studied something exceptional. Hence, during your most ineffective time, you learn the most exceptional things, which later become very useful. You can see from the history of science that **most inventions occurred accidentally during the most ineffective or idle time of the scientists.**

Hence, whenever you feel depressed, engage in some exceptional study and take the depression positively. However, the depression should not be excessive to affect your study and mind, and it should not persist for long.

Loneliness feelings

In the normal course, students live under the protection and support of parents in the home with the whole family. They share everything happening in their lives with all family members and feel protected when staying with other family members. However, when they are suddenly sent for exam preparation to a hostel hundreds of kilometres away from their home, they initially feel lonely. Most students adapt to hostel life, but a few cannot adjust to this new atmosphere. These homesick individuals further feel alone whenever they perform poorly in exams or during their examination period. The gravity of loneliness is more pronounced if the student is emotional and below-average in studies. They struggle to cope with the pressure of study and fall behind in each subject.

The top students adjust to hostel life because they find studies very interesting and can cope with the pressure of the supersonic speed of studies in class. They learn new things in the coaching classes; otherwise, they would have missed out if they had stayed in their hometown. This encourages them to enjoy hostel life for a bright future.

It is the duty of the parents, whenever their wards feel loneliness, to contact them daily on the phone and, if possible, to visit him or her once a month until he or she adjusts to hostel life. The students should try to form a group with other hostellers who can study or enjoy together. Parents should also seek feedback from other students about the behaviour of their son or daughter. It is the utmost duty of the parents to stay in touch with the friends of their wards to notice any behavioural changes in their nature. Otherwise, it would be very difficult for parents to control things once their children go into depression.

From the point of students, first, it is required that they should make a group of good friends of the same aptitude as they are, and they have to spend time together, study together, have meals together, and attend classes together. By spending time in a group, they will be saved from such depression.

Secondly, whenever you feel depressed and nostalgic about home, listen to some good religious songs (like bhajans) related to the God of your faith. Alternatively, watch motivational movies like *Chak De*, *The Karate Kid*, or any comedy movies or shows such as *Kapil Sharma Show* or *KBC* with Amitabh Bachchan. You can also read uplifting novels like *You Can Win* by Mr. Shiv Khera or watch YouTube channels featuring motivational speakers. These activities will make you feel lighter, encourage your studies, and dispel loneliness from your mind.

Once a day, during their free time, students should call their parents and share everything with them as if they were all living together at home. Parents should also inform their children about plan B in case they fail.

Here, I want to make a request to all parents that at whatever stage they feel their ward is under great depression, they should immediately rush to the hostel and tell other colleagues of their ward to take care of their ward until they reach the hostel. Here, don't ever think about how much money you have invested in your son's or daughter's education. This money is never more precious than the lives of your kids. One more thing, instead of staying in an individual rented room, it is better to stay in a hostel where at least 100 or more students are living together.

This chapter will be revisited in greater detail in Subchapter xiii of Main Chapter 45, where real-life examples of some renowned scientists will be discussed. While you may notice some repetition, remember that this is intentional. The aim is to help you better understand the significance of these moments of struggle, recognize the value hidden in periods of depression, and transform them into stepping stones for future success.

40

All Time Toppers

"Take the attitude of a student, never be too big to ask questions, never know too much to learn something new."

– Augustine Og Mandino

During my study and research at Kota, I found that there are three types of students who are committing suicide. First, those who are very emotional; second, those who are sent forcefully by their parents to study for entrance exams in Engineering, Medical, Law, or other fields; and third, those who were toppers throughout their lives and failed all of a sudden in an entrance exam.

The first category of students is those who are very touchy and emotional. They take everything to heart, and even a small comment from their parents, relatives, or neighbours can hurt them a lot. They tend to dwell on such comments for many days. Today, almost every student is more emotional compared to our generation 35 years ago. Parents need to handle them delicately so that their ego and self-respect are not hurt. At the same time, parents need to monitor their children's behaviour and reactions to every event in their lives, especially when they are living away from home. Therefore, parents can control such incidents of suicide. In such cases, parents can prevent more than 80% of suicide cases through timely action by informing their children about alternative plans.

The second category of students is those who are sent forcefully by their parents for entrance exams in Engineering, Medical, Law, etc., with the hope that one day they will become good engineers, doctors, lawyers, judges, etc., after studying at the best colleges in the country. It is the duty of the parents, before sending their children away from home, to ask politely whether their son or daughter wants to pursue such studies or not and whether they are going unwillingly due to parental pressure. Whether the field they are entering is truly their area of interest.

These questions should be asked separately by the mother, father, and elder siblings so that the student can openly discuss their feelings with at least one of them. If there is any reluctance from the student, then parents should immediately reconsider sending them away from home for such studies. They should only be sent when every family member, including the student, is in agreement.

Giving up on the idea of pushing your child into such competitions may cause temporary disappointment, but losing them forever will haunt you for the rest of your life, leaving you with a sense of guilt.

The third category of such cases is the students who were the toppers in their lives throughout and have never experienced failure. If they lose the battle, they are heavily hurt, especially emotionally. Generally, it is seen that there is very little competition in small towns. There are hardly 600 to 700 students in one class among all schools taken together. Hence, the competition is among these students only. Therefore, the topper of the town feels that there is no competition for him and no one to compete with.

But once they go away from their home for studying for such competitive exams, they find that the competition is among 1 million or more students rather than among 600 to 700 students. Places like Kota for entrance exams and Delhi for Civil Service examinations are oceans of competitions. Now, they have to fight with hundreds of thousands of students every year. If the student is able to cope with such pressure, then well and good; otherwise, they may experience depression because they have not seen defeat in their whole life. Failing in life is a very strange thing for them.

Hence, such students have to modify their target or increase the study hours or effort for such competition. The day they feel depression after seeing such competition, they have to immediately seek help from their tutors of coaching class, explain everything to their parents, and decide on a further course of action. Timely action at this initial phase is very much required to save the lives of many students every year. Hence, parents have to think ten times before sending their wards for study away from home if he or she falls into one of the three categories given below:

1. If they are very emotional and touchy,
2. If they are not keen to go for study, and parents are sending them forcefully,
3. If they were toppers throughout their lives in a small town and have not seen a single failure in their lives.

41

Unlocking English: Simple Steps to Strong Writing

"If it makes you nervous, you're doing it right."

– Childish Gambino

Generally, Hindi medium students or non-English medium students who are appearing in the Civil Services examination or state PSC, often find difficulty in writing essays or narrative answers. Hence, it is very useful for them to read a few novels written by Mr. Khushwant Singh, Mr. Chetan Bhagat, or by any other good author who uses very simple English in their books. This practice will give them confidence in writing answers in exams with fluent English in an artistic way. These authors use very simple English, especially for Indian readers. The flow of English in their novels is exceptional.

All students, especially after attaining maturity, must read novels to learn how to write English. All such novels are beneficial for learning English, especially for Hindi medium students or non-English medium students.

For further improving your English, just make two copies: one for writing the meanings with the usage of words in sentences, and the other for noting down any good information, data, or quotes you find in any newspaper. The information, quotes, or data can be used in writing answers to narrative-type questions to impress the evaluator.

Remember or revise these two copies after a gap of 2 weeks so that you will not need to read them during the exam periods. This way, you can easily recall this information or these meanings whenever you need to write in the exam.

Always use a good dictionary in which the meaning of any word is explained in different contexts. By reading and using these words repeatedly, you will gain a good command of English. Such dictionary is generally helpful in understanding multiple meaning of any word and recommended for Hindi medium or non-English medium students because they are weak in English.

42

Value of Money and Time

"It is a rough road that leads to the heights of greatness."

– Lucius Annaeus Seneca

Just go back to the 1980s or before when all exam forms were filled out in hard copies, and exams were conducted offline using hard copies. During that time, letters were written to various institutes, and fees were deposited for forms through demand drafts. Subsequently, the exam forms were received, filled out, and sent with a demand draft for the exam fee to various entrance exam centres. Admit cards were then received just a week before the exams.

For the students of a small town like Panna, the condition was more pathetic. We had to go to Rewa or Jabalpur to purchase forms or to appear in exams because there were only a few exam centres. The process was lengthy and time-consuming, but we realised the value of time and money. We used to go to the bank for form fees or exam fees, to get a demand draft after taking money from our parents. The only thing our parents were aware of was that their son or daughter had asked for a few rupees for an exam, and nothing else. They were not even aware of the name of the exam, the date, or the purpose of our participation. They only found out on the day we got selected.

Now, the conditions have changed; the world is moving very fast today. Things have reversed. Parents are searching for how many colleges (Engineering, Medical, Law, or Humanities) are available, the dates for filling up the forms, and the dates for appearing in these exams. This way, their kids can devote all their energy and time to studying only, and their minds are not diverted by secondary things.

Nowadays, there are many college entrance exams that you can take from home, while a few require you to go to designated centres. There are also specific exams where you must attend on selected days, but only at government-approved or affiliated centres online.

Due to these multiple exams such as JEE (Mains), VIT, BITSAT, etc., for Engineering, NEET and AIIMS for Medical studies, and CLAT for Law, students are generally busy from January to May every year.

We can see from the results that the selection of slightly poor students is higher compared to rich and pampered kids. The students who belong to the middle class also score better because of their hardworking nature. The poor kids score better because they can't afford the fees of various exams, so they fully dedicate their energy in selected exams as they have only a few exams to appear in.

The students who search various exams and colleges for their career and fill up the forms themselves realise the value of money and time. Hence, parents have to let them fill up the forms themselves and pay from their own pocket money. Although parents can reimburse the money spent on exams later, or the students can go to a nearby online centre in the market to fill up various exam forms and pay the person sitting at the desk.

If you as parents are filling up their form online, then let your kids sit with you alongside so that they will learn the value of time and money. I am recommending this strategy to generate a sense of responsibility in the minds of your kids. They will realise how hard it is for their parents to earn money.

Today, parents are more tense in searching for colleges and filling out forms for each one. Kids are not aware of which form or exam their parents have filled out. They don't know the efforts and time spent by parents on these activities.

Kids are highly pampered today, even in the middle class; hence, they are unaware of the efforts of parents. Therefore, they must learn about the energy spent by their parents on their career.

The students who are down to earth and have financial constraints are more successful because they have limited means, limited exams, and limited options. Thus, they spend all their energy on the selected few exams only.

43

Old System of PET and PMT

"If there is no struggle, there is no progress."

– Frederick Douglass

Prior to the era of NEET and JEE (Mains), there were exams conducted by States as well. However, due to corruption in a few states regarding entrance exams for Medical and Engineering, the Central Government initiated a centralised system of examination for Medical and Engineering etc. Each state used to conduct two main examinations: PET (Pre-Engineering Test) for Bachelor of Engineering, Architecture, or Polytechnic, and PMT (Pre-Medical Test) for MBBS, BDS, Veterinary, and BAMS.

There were seats reserved for REC (Regional Engineering College, now known as NIT National Institute of Technology) for students of other States. In one sense, the system was good because competition was limited to one state only; hence, the competition was among only a few thousand students instead of 1 million students today. The syllabus was based on the state education board; hence, it was easy for even below-average students to get into an average Engineering or Medical College. Now, state board students have to compete pan-India with CBSE and ICSE boards' students.

When the students were competing in the state, they were aware of the intellectual level of the other students in the same state and the level of the syllabus. Mental levels of students vary drastically when comparing students from two States. So, it is better to delegate that power back to the states for conducting entrance exams for Engineering and Medical. It will be a better move towards the decentralisation of power as outlined in the Constitution of India. JEE will be the only exam for IITs nationwide, in a single stage without wasting time on two examinations like Mains and Advanced. Similarly, for Medicals, only AIIMS shall be conducted nationwide exclusively for AIIMS colleges, not for other colleges, and NEET shall be delegated back to states like PMT in the past.

By adopting this system, the depression among students will be reduced, and there will be chances of getting selected in at least a few Engineering or Medical colleges in the states even for average students. Competing among 80,000 students and among 1.2 million students makes a great difference. In the 1980s and 1990s, we hardly heard of any cases of suicide. The reason lies in the analogy of swimming in a pond versus swimming in an ocean. **The fear of swimming in the ocean is much greater than swimming in a small pond.** Sometimes, this fear leads the students towards depression.

44

Curiosity Pays

"People often say that motivation doesn't last. Well, neither does bathing – that's why we recommend it daily."

– Zig Ziglar

Curiosity is the desire to learn. It's an eagerness to explore, discover, and figure things out. Have you noticed that in every class, some students are especially interested in learning new things? They often become topics of discussion, as others might mock or misunderstand their enthusiasm, labeling them as unusual or even dull. However, these students are often far from dim-witted; many are exceptional.

By the time these curious students graduate from high school or college, they often surprise their peers with impressive achievements, such as acceptance into top colleges or landing exceptional jobs due to their inquisitive nature.

Why do these students achieve so much success in academics? Let's explore the reasons behind their achievements in detail.

As we've discussed various inferiority complexes in other chapters, shyness about curiosity can be another complex that affects some students. Often, due to teasing, these students may become reserved, but they continue to study diligently, giving their best to their academic pursuits.

To develop curiosity, a solid base of knowledge is essential. Curiosity leads to questions, but to ask insightful questions, you need a good understanding of fundamental concepts; otherwise, it may backfire. These students ask questions in class, which are answered by teachers or classmates, allowing them to deepen their understanding and retain information longer.

Curious students often enhance their memory by actively engaging with information. Here's why it works:

When we read a topic in a newspaper or book, our first reading is often casual, and we may remember the general content without specific details like figures or unique information (e.g., names or dates). But when we revisit that topic, focusing on these unique details, they stick in our memory. If we read them again after a day or two, they can remain in our memory much longer, possibly even permanently.

Let's clarify with an example. Suppose there's a headline in the Business Times that reads, "Sensex falls by 690 points, closes at 76,950." In the first reading, you may understand the context but not remember these specific figures because the article is filled with additional details like the reasons for the Sensex drop, the behaviours of various companies' share prices and selling by foreign Institutional investors etc.

Your attention is often drawn to the reasoning rather than specific numbers or details. To remember these figures, you need to revisit them and focus on memorizing them.

To improve memory, a topic needs three readings:

1. **First reading:** Understand the facts and reasoning of the topic.
2. **Second reading:** Immediately review specific values, figures, or unique information to retain them longer.
3. **Third reading:** After a day or two, read again to make the information more permanent in memory.

You may wonder why I'm discussing this in relation to curiosity. Here's the connection:

These three readings represent the benefit of a single query raised by a curious student. When they ask a question, it's a specific inquiry directed toward a teacher or friend, which imprints the information in their memory more deeply than a passive reading. This is also why group study can be advantageous for entrance exams in Engineering, Medical, or for Civil Services exams.

When a teacher explains something in response to a question, it tends to stay longer in the memory of curious students. Thus, those who ask questions often have a clearer understanding and a longer retention of information than others.

So, the next time you feel a question bubbling up inside you, don't be afraid to ask. Your curiosity is not a weakness—it's a strength. And when you see your curiosity as a strength, it will certainly pay you in the aspects you might not have thought of yet.

45

Irrelevant But Relevant

"I do not try to dance better than anyone else. I only try to dance better than myself."

– Arianna Huffington

There is a delicate yet significant difference between wasting and investing. As parents, we often believe that the money we spend on our children's education and upbringing is an investment in their bright future. But imagine, just for a moment, if that money was not an investment but a risk, a gamble with no guarantee of return. Think that the entire money is simply gone, or vanished from your savings.

Now, imagine the joy and relief when, years later, that "wasted" money returns to you tenfold as a well-rounded, successful adult—your child. What once seemed like a gamble is now an investment that has given you 10X returns.

It is all about perspective.

Consider something as simple as an air conditioner (AC). To some, it's just a machine that cools the room, a luxury item. But for others, it can be a tool that provides the comfort needed to study for three extra hours, turning late nights into productive ones. It's about how you choose to see and utilize what you have.

The same logic applies to the movies you watch or the books you read. Watch ten movies, and you might just have the insight to create the 11th. Read ten books, and you might find yourself inspired to write the 11th.

While children gear up for their career, we as parents we need to do a reality check: Why are there more suicide cases among students aged 16 to 20, those preparing for Medical or Engineering entrances, compared to those aged 20 to 25 preparing for Civil Services?

The first reason is maturity—the older group has more life experience to handle pressure. The second reason is the sense of security that comes from having a degree—a safety net that can catch them if they fall. The very act of preparing for the Civil Services exams brings a sense of confidence, a belief that even if they don't succeed in one area, they have the skills and knowledge to succeed elsewhere. This is a confidence that students in the earlier age group, still finding their footing, often lack.

Ultimately, it's not just about the money we spend or the tools we provide to our children—it's about the mindset we cultivate in them. With the right perspective and support, what may seem like a gamble today can turn into the greatest investment of all: a resilient, confident, and successful future for our children.

There are 14 sub-chapters below to offer you more personal guidance and inspiration in your journey.

i. *Role of the Pen and Refilling the Pen*

A similar strategy to lighting up an Incense Stick (Agarbatti) is the emptying or using up of a pen's refill or cartridge. After each study session or writing notes, I would observe the ink level of the pen's refill. Using the refill brings satisfaction, motivating us to study more and prompting us to buy a new one. This constant cycle encourages us to extend our study hours and build our study stamina. Upon finishing a refill, we are usually motivated to purchase a new one.

Today, the pens are disposable, and we don't refill these pens. Hence, the purchase of a new pen is a great encouragement to study further.

Remember one thing that the flow of the pen or the smoothness in writing matters a lot during the examination as well as during study at home or at the classroom. It matters more for the subjective papers. Generally, we are engrossed in deep thinking whenever replying to the narrative answers because whatever we think in the mind, immediately the pen in hand writes everything on the answer sheet.

There is hardly any time-lag between the thoughts processing in the mind and writing by pen. But once our pen interrupts in writing or if the flow is not proper, then immediately that thought or trick vanishes from our mind, and the reply for that question distorts. In the case of numerical questions, we generally commit a mistake and write the wrong answer for the numerical problems.

Now, you can imagine how much a small fault of the pen can cost you, especially for Civil Services or other entrance exams. In situations where there are 10 to 15 candidates with the same marks, a mistake of few marks can drop your rank from 50 to 150.

Always use a good quality pen with a smooth flow of ink and smoothness in writing. Ensure you have a good grip with your three fingers (including thumb) so that your handwriting will be clear and legible. This is particularly important for numerical questions in Maths, Physics, or Chemistry, as well as for writing narrative or subjective answers in exams.

ii. *Tame a Pet or Keep Birds, etc.*

During my posting in Kota, the suicide cases were very regularly seen every fortnight in the newspapers. Such incidents were very heart-touching for me. To prevent such cases and to understand the post-suicide conditions of the family members, I would suggest to all emotional students to adopt a pet like a dog, rabbit, cat, or any bird such as a parrot, lovebirds, or a cute mouse. After a few days, you would be so attached to that animal or bird that you cannot live without it.

You will start playing with it, you will be worried whether it has taken a meal or not, and whether there is sufficient water for it in the utensils.

One of my friends, Mr. Pankaj Saxena, told me during the stay in Jia Sarai, Delhi, that after long usage, we generally become attached to non-living things as well. If we lose that article or non-living thing, we also feel very hurt. Such attachments usually take months or years in the case of non-living things, but in the case of human beings, animals, or birds, we can become attached within one day. Parents are attached even before our birth, when we are inside the wombs of our mothers. Parents' love is the most pure, precious, and selfless love without any expectations in return.

If your pet is attached with you, and you are also attached to that pet, and one day it dies, then just imagine your feelings.

How hurt you feel on that day, even though you have not given birth to that pet or bird; you just purchased it from the market or brought it from any street or jungle. A few days of attachment gives you so much sorrow or sadness after its death. Now, imagine yourself as the pet and your parents in your place. Just imagine the condition of your family members if you commit such crimes. If you could imagine the condition of your parents, then you will never commit such a crime.

Committing suicide is a crime not only against you, but also against God and your parents. If you could see a film or a scene in a film depicting the aftermath at home after this act, I am sure you would never consider such a step in your life. Just imagine, who will take care of your parents or family members in old age? The situation would be even more distressing if you are the only child to care for your parents in their old age.

I would request all the emotional students, whenever they are in standard 6th or 7th, to tame a pet or keep some birds if they are staying with their parents. They will realise the value of relations or attachments once they lose that pet or bird. Then, they will never commit such crimes in the future.

iii. *Success Rate Now (2020s) and Then (1980s).*

Here I am comparing the success rate of students in the 1980s and 2020s with respect to the medium of language. In the 1980s, the success rate of vernacular language students was much higher compared to English medium students because of a shortage of English medium schools in small towns. In Civil Services, as well as in Engineering and Medical Entrance exams, the representation of Hindi medium students or other regional language students was more than it is today.

Vernacular language is the language used by the people in day-to-day speaking. Generally, these vernacular students have an inferiority complex when they compare themselves with the English medium students. But I assure you that the success rate will be higher if a vernacular student's medium of instruction in school is also their vernacular language. Because if your mother tongue is the same as the medium in school, then 100% of your energy will go towards understanding concepts. However, if your mother tongue is different from the school's medium, a larger part of your energy will be spent on translating English to the vernacular language and vice versa. There is a background translator in our mind that converts vernacular language into English or English to the vernacular language.

Our thoughts are formed in vernacular language in our mind, so there is a time lag between the thought formation in vernacular language and then speaking in English, and similarly understanding English and then converting into vernacular language. The translation costs a lot if your mother tongue and medium are not the same language. It matters more for humanities or arts subjects than for science subjects.

English is also a necessity in life because it is the language of every software in a computer, and one day or the other, everyone has to go abroad for higher study or for a job; hence, we cannot ignore this language. Therefore, we have to make a balance between English and our mother tongue so that there will not be any inferiority complex in the minds of vernacular students. At the same time, our job or study will be smooth in foreign countries. One day, this inferiority complex will vanish when you realise that English is just a language or medium; it has nothing to do with smartness.

Another inferiority complex which is present in students from small towns or villages is that they may not be as smart as students from metropolitan areas. However, these students are often more successful compared to their metropolitan counterparts. This is evidenced every year by the results of Civil Services examinations, JEE, NEET, etc.

The students from small towns or villages should not worry about this matter because smartness hardly matters in the written exams. Its role comes during the interview only, but if your knowledge base is strong, then you can overcome this during the interview as well. In an interview, knowledge and smartness both matter, and only smartness cannot do anything without knowledge. However, less smartness can be compensated with in-depth knowledge.

The success rate is also high among the students who live a life with mild poverty compared to affluent individuals who have all sorts of luxuries. The elite class students are generally pampered, and they don't realise the value of money. These wealthy individuals have everything in their lives for which less privileged individuals work hard and study more. These affluent individuals don't have ambitions for becoming rich because they already have every luxury in their lives. The only ambition they have is to protect the empire given by their parents and, if possible, to expand it.

Hence, students who belong to average families or live in mild poverty are generally more successful in Engineering and

Medical Entrance exams, or in Civil Services examinations because they understand the value of each penny earned by their parents and aim to overcome poverty in their lives.

iv. *Need for Career Counselling Agencies (CCA) in India*

There are coaching classes fully devoted to academics, and psychologists who focus on psychology. Here we need the Career Counselling Agencies in India which can take care both aspects. The students and parents can seek help from these Career Counselling Agencies to decide on the future or career path of the students. These agencies will guide the students after serving a questionnaire to them, and based on their replies, these agencies will suggest to the students and their parents what field will be better for their wards. Although the decision of the students or even the parents will be final, these agencies will assist the parents in deciding the most appropriate field for the student.

These Career Counselling Agencies can charge a nominal amount as a membership fee for the first-time visit, and they will provide consultancy for choosing a career for the student. For further visits, they will charge for any specific career queries.

The purpose of the CCA Start-ups will be manifold.

Generally, coaching centres and schools devote all their time to academics. Parents in India often avoid visiting psychologists due to societal perceptions. Therefore, CCA will serve as a link between these two. Cases of depression and suicide can be reduced by choosing the right career path based on the calibre of the students. Depression may arise when students select the wrong stream under parental pressure or set targets beyond their capacity or talent. These factors contribute to suicide cases in Kota.

Many a time, it is seen that under the pressure of parents, students adopt Engineering or Medical as their career path. They may struggle to express their true desires to their parents regarding their preferred field. However, CCA can assist in these situations.

Whatever the students cannot dare to tell their parents, that can be expressed to these agencies. The final consultancy of these agencies can be helpful for deciding the future and career of these students. Hence, these CCAs can work as a channel between the students and their parents to express the opinions of the wards to their parents. So, the stage of depression and, finally, suicide can be stopped here only, and the students will go to the field where they desired to go. There will not be any undue pressure from the parents to choose the specific stream for these students.

The help of CCA can be sought at any stage after 8th standard, after 11th standard, or after 12th standard, or even after graduation for consultancy and guidance. It can also be helpful to seek such guidance during the 6th standard if their child is mature enough to understand such counselling.

These CCAs shall be affiliated with schools and coaching classes, and they must visit the schools and coaching classes monthly or quarterly to promote or motivate the students so that the students can avoid falling into depression due to academic pressure. Such CCAs are very much required in Kota, where four lakh students are studying every year for Engineering and Medical entrance exams.

Presently, there is no such agency like CCA, but there are motivational speakers, and their lectures or speeches are available on YouTube. Hence, this field is unorganised and unstructured, and they are not targeted specifically to the students and their careers. Hence, we need more streamlined agencies which will be specific to the needs of the students, and these will be available whenever students demand them for consultancy.

These CCAs shall have good motivational speakers in their panels, or they can call successful candidates of Civil Service examination, JEE, or NEET as guest faculty to guide the students. These CCAs can also show inspirational movies to the students of coaching classes and schools.

I hope that by the introduction of the concept of CCA in India, the cases of depression, and ultimately suicide, among students will be eliminated completely.

v. *Reading Newspapers and Magazines*

During the preparation of Engineering; Medical, or any other entrance exams, students don't have time to read newspapers or magazines because they are fully occupied with studying the syllabus of 11th and 12th grades and solving test papers for competitive exams. However, if they plan to appear for the Civil Services examination, Engineering Services examination, or any competition for job, it is advisable to start reading newspapers from the 6th standard.

Hence as a student, you can dedicate at least 15 minutes daily to read a good newspaper to stay updated on current affairs; this practice offers multiple benefits.

- You will gain a good command over any language, and your writing skill will improve.
- Your knowledge of current affairs will improve.
- The newspaper has a good inspirational and motivational force, so you will be inspired to crack any competitive exam.
- The newspapers publish the interviews of successful candidates in Civil Service examinations, JEE, or NEET every year. You can take guidance from the successful candidates. Some of the tricks or strategies of the successful candidates can be very helpful for your career.

If you are very busy in the class study or in any other exam, then at least flip over the pages of newspapers and read only the headlines or the topics of your interest. The next part is the editorial in the newspaper that will be very useful if you are appearing in any exam which has General Knowledge or General Study as a paper. If you want to appear in Civil Services examination, then at a very early stage, you have to make a habit of reading the newspaper and a magazine, although it may be a cursory reading in the early years.

For Civil Services aspirants, I suggest reading the newspaper daily after the 6th standard because the Civil Service examination asks many questions based on current affairs. The CSE exam includes many subjective papers; therefore, by reading the newspaper, you will be able to write good essays or narrative answers for the General Study paper. This practice is also helpful for interviews due to your updated knowledge of national and international news.

Similarly, choose a good monthly magazine to read that is related to your career. If you want to go into the finance field, then read the Business Times one page in any newspaper.

vi. *No Cheating Please*

Here I want to tell you the real-life story of 1982 when I was in standard 5th. At that time, I was scared of subjects like languages (Hindi, English) and Humanities, but I was fond of subjects such as Maths, Biology, etc. According to your interest in various subjects, teachers also like or dislike you. There are three groups of students in the minds of every teacher as per their likings. If the teacher is teaching Science or Maths and if you are also inclined to those subjects, then you are in his or her good books. Other two groups are the neutral group and the non-liking group. If you are not performing well in the field of the teacher's interest, then he or she may not like you. It is quite possible that if you are at the top of the liking list of one teacher, then you may be in the neutral list or non-liking list of another teacher.

There are few exceptions among the students as well as among the teachers. Some teachers love each and every student equally, similarly, some students who are all-rounders are liked by all teachers, but such students are the rarest of rare species. They cannot be all-rounders in graduation because they have to choose any one of the streams, either Science or Humanities. The performance of these all-rounder students generally deteriorates compared to the performance of students specialising in a specific stream during various entrance exams or during graduation.

Being an all-rounder throughout your life is very difficult to maintain. The chances of experiencing depression for these individuals are very high because they have never encountered failure in their earlier years and may struggle to adapt to it.

I was also not an exception to this concept, as I was inclined towards science subjects. Hence, I was liked by the teachers who taught Maths, Science, etc., but not liked by the teachers who taught me Humanities subjects or languages. Another preference shown by teachers was for students who were the sons or daughters of teachers or high-ranking officers. I fell into neither category. The parents of these two groups of students frequently met with the class teachers and the school principal. Considering all of the above, I was always scared if any teacher from my school came to my house.

The reasons were many. The average age of parents was 40 years for all my classmates, but my parents were nearly 50 when I was in standard V. My mother was 8th pass, and my father was only 5th pass. They were not as smart as other parents. I was their 5th child among all siblings (my five sisters and me); only one sister was younger than me. My elder sister got married before my birth, and her first son was even older than me. I was full of this complex that my parents were not well-educated and smart compared to other parents.

Another reason that I never invited my teachers home was that I was a "full of tantrum" guy. There was no restriction on me for anything because I was the only son among all siblings, so I was scared that my sisters or my parents would complain to my teachers.

The last reason was that my partitioned house was very small, and we only had one room to accommodate five members in 1982. My two sisters had gotten married, and my father was living in the common hall with other elderly members of the joint family. The room was so cramped that I never invited any teacher on my own.

The houses of the parents, those who were teachers or officers in Panna, were very big and clean. Hence, I always used to compare my house with theirs, and in that complex, I never invited any teacher or principal for dinner or otherwise.

One fine evening, three nun teachers arrived at my home for a surprise visit while I was sleeping at 5:00 p.m. In a hurry, we shifted three tables and five chairs to my room, and we offered them snacks and tea. I was shivering during their visit because I was scared that my mother or any of the sisters might have mentioned my fighting nature. I was a pampered child without any luxury, but everything went well. That day, my three teachers came to know about my financial condition, and they became sympathetic towards me throughout my education in that school.

You may be wondering why I shared the above story. Aren't you? It may seem irrelevant to you at first, but let's take another look at the title of the 45th chapter: "Irrelevant But Relevant." The first part of my story might not seem important to you, but the second part carries a valuable lesson. It's about how I once tried to cheat on a test and how that experience changed my life forever, teaching me never to take such shortcuts again.

If you take the time to practice writing answers to all the questions at home, you won't ever need to copy or cheat during an exam. A small incident like this can change your whole life, just as it did for me, by teaching you an important lesson.

The first part of this sub-chapter also shows you how disciplined and respectful we were towards our teachers in the 1980s. Back then, the fear of our teachers played a crucial role in shaping us into disciplined individuals, not just during our school days but throughout our lives.

In the schools, we were also very scared of the teachers in case of non-completion of homework, a poor score in the test, or not replying to any query by the teacher. They used to beat students with a stick or a wooden ruler, but only on the thin edge, never on the blunt or flat side of the ruler.

One day, my teacher, Mrs Asha Shrivastava (we generally called her Asha behen ji), taught a chapter on Malaria. On that day, I was absent. Generally, there was a terror in the school about her nature. The next day when I went to school, she announced that there would be a test on that chapter. I was sure I would be beaten up by her if I performed poorly in the test that would be conducted the very next day. After going home, I was upset for a few minutes. Then I decided to cheat in the exam, but the issue was how to cheat in a class of only twenty-three students. After pondering for an hour, an idea came to my mind. I decided to write all the questions and the answers in the test copy of that subject on the last blank pages. There were hardly 10 small questions and answers of that chapter, which was covered in 3-4 pages. Just to avoid the insult in class, I took another bigger risk of cheating.

The next day, I appeared in the class test in the month of December 1982. The class teacher started dictating the ten questions to reply to in 30 minutes. After every question, I felt happy because I had the readymade solution for each question. After 10 minutes, when she finished dictating all ten questions, we started writing the answers. After 25 minutes of writing, I found that I did not need to refer to the opening of the last pages for reference or cheating because during the writing of these 10 questions at home, I remembered each and every word or line of the answer. I never flipped to the last pages to see that answer during those 30 minutes. I could recall whatever I wrote on the last pages of my copy.

That was the first and the last unsuccessful cheating in an exam for me, and I learned a big lesson. **If you want anything to last longer in your memory, try writing answers at home for the exam.** It will clarify your concepts and engrave them in your memory forever. In lower classes, you can cheat to pass exams, but in senior classes, the syllabus is too vast for cheating.

No one can be successful in the long run by adopting shortcuts. Hence, always try to write the answer many times at home so that exam fear will vanish from your mind, and the mistakes you commit at home will not be repeated in the exam.

vii. *The Old Golden Days and Today's Overburdened Kids*

If we want to know the reason behind the increasing incidences of suicide cases today among the students, then we have to compare the conditions of today's kids with the conditions of the kids of the 1980s or 1990s. Today, the kids are overburdened with the pressure of study, whether it may be excessive number of books, fewer holidays, long duration of coaching hours, and other academic or non-academic activities like projects in schools.

In the golden old days, there was a limited syllabus and a limited number of books to study. There were State Boards and a Central Education Board, each with a limited selection of specific books for every subject. There were mainly two types of entrance exams: one for the State Board's syllabus, i.e. PET or PMT and the other for the Central Board's syllabus, i.e. JEE or AIIMS. Mainly, the Engineering or Medical colleges were run by the state or the central governments.

Now there are many reputed private Engineering and Medical colleges like BITS, VIT, SRM, KIT. Some are conducting their own exams, and some are accepting the score of JEE. During my time, I appeared only in two exams: one for PET and another for BIT BHILAI. So I devoted my whole energy to these two exams, and the syllabus and the pattern were the same for these two entrance exams, and I got selected in both of these exams. I also filled up the form for IIT entrance (JEE), but due to different syllabus and pattern as well as less gap between board exams and JEE, I did not appear in JEE at that time in 1990.

Today, students fill out at least ten forms for various entrance exams, all of which are held within 2 months. Hence, they hardly have a gap of 10 days to prepare for each exam. It is very difficult to switch from one exam to another as each exam has its own pattern and syllabus. Some exams include English questions, while others may have logical reasoning. Therefore, students struggle to concentrate due to the multiple exams and may experience depression if they do not perform well in any of them.

Here, the government has to intervene so that there will be only one exam – JEE for Engineering, either NEET or AIIMS for medical, and every college has to accept the score of these tests only. No other score will be valid, like in GMAT, SAT, GRE, etc.

In the 1980s, there was hardly any culture of coaching classes. Schools were imparting sufficient educational inputs to students to qualify the board exams and the entrance exam for Engineering and Medical. At that time, students were living with their parents in joint families, and there was no culture of hostel life before graduation. We only went to the hostel during our graduation. Hence, because of the joint family or staying with parents, the chances of going into depression were very low, and because of that, there were no cases of suicide in the 1980s. In the case of depression due to poor scores or failure, someone, maybe a father, uncle, or elder brother was there to console us, so we felt supported even in the case of a poor score or failure in any exam.

In the 1980s, there were long vacations during Diwali, Christmas (winter vacation after the half-yearly exams), and in summer (vacation after the final exams). At that time, students had a lot of free time due to limited books and syllabus. However, today, students have to attend school classes just after the final exam of the previous class and are burdened with homework given for the next two months of summer vacation. Hence, students do not feel that they have the free time for joy and fun after the exam, as we did after every final exam of any class in the 1980s. Earlier, it was our choice to study the next class syllabus during the summer vacation, and it was not compulsory.

It basically depended on us whether we wanted to study the next year's syllabus or not. Today, it is compulsory to read the next year's syllabus.

Earlier, we used to go to other cities to Nana-nani's house, Mama-mami's house, or to our sister's house. The metro's guys enjoyed the village life, and the village guys used to enjoy metro life at Nana-nani's house during summer vacation. It was complete fun in those two months of summer vacation. During this period, we enjoyed icecream, lassi, ice-gola, mango shake, masti in parks, mangoes by pelting stones on the tree, chaat, and golgappe. But all these things have vanished from the lives of students today. Their lives have confined to a few books and a room of coaching class in isolation, giving rise to a feeling of depression. It is because of the heavy competitions that are pan-India, which were earlier confined to a state only.

Today, there are many books published by various publishers and written by different authors. Students are entangled among these books and could not finish even one, unlike us. Due to the limited syllabus and few books in the 1980s, we could revise each book at least four times a year. Hence, our concepts were very clear by reading the same book repeatedly.

In a few coaching centres, there are ten or more tests conducted by the teachers every month. Consequently, students are busy taking tests only, and they are not able to devote time to study. In the old times, there was only one test for each subject every month, and that too within two to three days for all subjects. This meant that for the remaining 27 days, we were free to study and clarify concepts in Science or Maths subjects.

In 1980, we were engaging in physical activities like roaming around the city or village, swimming in the pond, or visiting various places during the summer vacation. We truly enjoyed our childhood. The only thing our parents considered bad was reading comics or novels, which was actually beneficial as it enhanced our language skills and writing abilities. However, today, Mobiles, the internet, YouTube, and WhatsApp have replaced comics and novels. Consequently, instead of reading or writing, the students now devote more time to audio books or video clips. The joy of reading comics or novels can only be appreciated by the kids of the 1980s. It was truly an amazing experience to read comics or novels during lunch or dinner in the summer vacation.

In the 1980s, parents were not involved in the study of students. We never sought the help of our parents in academics or school activities. Today, parents are more tense than students during their tests or exams in schools.

In the 1980s, there were only academics in the schools or any cultural or sports meet, and that too once a year. But today, apart from that, every student is given multiple project activities. Although they are useful for the practical knowledge of students, in reality, they are made by the parents instead of by the kids themselves.

Here we need to remove the excessive burden on the students by limiting their syllabus, books, and study hours, giving power to the states for colleges within that state, conducting only one exam at the centre, and the score of that will be valid for all colleges under the Central Government.

viii. Some More Insults

Here, I want to quote a few incidents from my life where I felt very insulted in front of the whole class. It hardly matters before the teenage, but when we enter the sensitive age of teenage, we feel very humiliated once insulted by anyone in front of others. Such humiliations may be because of a poor score, failure in an exam, or committing any mistake, or otherwise.

First such incident happened to me in my school when I was in 4th standard in 1981. One day, our English teacher told us to write an essay on "Padosi" (we call a neighbour 'Padosi' in Hindi).

The issue was that I was not aware of the English word for "Padosi," and I did not have the dictionary (Hindi to English). So, I asked my papa to find out the English word for it. When my papa was going to the market to meet his other colleagues, I gave him a slip with the Hindi word "Padosi" written on it.

After 1 hour, when he came back from the market, he gave me that slip in which the word "NEIGHBOUR" was written. It was given to him by one of his friends who was slightly acquainted with English.

But it was only written on the slip, so neither my papa nor I was aware of how to pronounce it. At that time, phones were also not popular; hence, I could not ask how to pronounce it. As I asked my papa to get only the English word for it, he also forgot to ask its actual pronunciation. At 9:00 p.m., I started writing an essay on neighbours. Within 40 minutes, I finished writing it, and according to my standard, it was the best essay I could write as a student of Hindi medium.

The next day in the class, the teacher checked the essays of all students. Mine was just an okay type of writing, but it appeared to her that it was written by me with abstract language without the help of anyone.

There were some students whose parents were teachers or officers. They took the help of their parents, and it was clearly visible to our class teacher that they had taken the help of their parents. She randomly selected my copy and told me to read it out loudly so that others could also listen.

As I was not aware of its exact pronunciation, hence as a layman, I pronounced it as "ney-gh-bur" instead of "ney-bu." The whole class started laughing at me, but my class teacher realised where I committed a mistake due to the unique feature of English pronunciation. She mildly smiled, corrected my mistake, and told me it is pronounced as "ney-bu," not as "ney-gh-bur;" here "gh" and "r" are both silent.

As we learn from our mistakes and always try to improve, hence it was a good incidence for me to improve it, and later I decided to buy a dictionary. Finally, I bought that dictionary during Diwali vacation when I won money in gambling on the night of Diwali.

The next similar incident happened when I was selected as a monitor, and I asked my sister-in-law what we called 'Vigyan' in English. She told me it is known as "science" and pronounced as 'sI-un(t)s.' Then, applying my Hindi to English translator, in my mind, I made the spelling, and the next day in school, I wrote "SINSE" on the blackboard during the science period.

Passing through the class, three teachers saw the spelling written by me on the board. They started laughing and asked the whole class who had written it. I raised my hand as it was the duty of the monitor to clear the board and write the name of the next subject on the top of the blackboard. It was very embarrassing for me, and one of the teachers corrected the spelling of science.

These two incidents happened when I was hardly 11 years old. So, hardly did I feel humiliated for a few minutes, then I decided to move on by ignoring both incidents.

The next incident happened when I was in 9th class. At that time, I used to sit in my shop and always kept some books to read during free time. There was a book for NTSE, published for the talent search exam conducted by NCERT. Then one day, the head of the royal family, Late Shri Narendra Singh Ji, came to my shop and asked me to show that book. I gave that to him, and he found three mistakes in the full form of NCERT. I had written Concil instead of Council, Resurch instead of Research, and Traning instead of Training. It was during my teenage years. I felt very humiliated because of my age. Then he asked me who had told me to write such mistakes in English. I was so scared that I mentioned the name of my English teacher, Mr. Qureshi, although the mistakes were committed by me.

The book was in Hindi, but I wrote the full form of NCERT as pronounced in the village for Council, Research, and Training. Again, it was a good lesson for me to read, write and remember the correct spelling of each word so that errors could be eliminated in drafting English.

The next issue was related to the extension of my school from class 5th to class 8th. My school only went up to class 5th until 1983, and the following year we were supposed to graduate from that school. Since it was a highly reputed school in Panna, we endeavoured to have it extended up to 8th class. Eventually, permission was granted by the Bishop of Satna, allowing us to continue studying in that school up to 8th class.

Now came the issue of fund for the construction of an additional room for the next 3 years so that our class will sit in a new room each year for the next 3 years. The school administration started collecting the funds from all the beneficiaries for these additional classes. The main beneficiaries were the students of our class, so every student's parents contributed, ranging from Rs. 50 to Rs. 1000. Some parents committed that they would give cement worth rupees 1000; some committed sand, bricks, iron rods, or girders for the construction of the classrooms.

The class teacher-cum-principal, Sister Christina, also asked me to donate something. I asked my father to give some money as a donation. He told me that our cousin brother had already given Rs. 50 as a donation, so there was no need because ours was a joint family and we used to go to school together.

Next day, my teacher asked me where my donation was. I replied that my family had already given Rs. 50 for it, so I am not giving separately. Then she replied that it was given by your cousin's family, not by your parents. This was told by her in front of the whole class of twenty-three students when I was in standard 5th. It was a very embarrassing condition for me, not because of academics, but because of my poor financial condition.

Just before few days hardly I could manage to purchase the dictionary and it was very difficult to pay fees in the joint family. The biggest challenge in the joint family was that the **resources**

are distributed equally among all the members, even though which are earned or created by only a few active members. My father struggled to arrange the fees, book expenses, and uniform costs after managing the joint family expenses.

I am just quoting these two types of insults or embarrassments just to explain the contrast between insults in teenage and insults before teenage. Before teenage, we are generally not so emotional; hence, we can absorb such incidences of insults in the class or elsewhere. But when we enter the teenage years, we get too emotional; hence, it is very difficult to forget such incidences. We carry them for many days in our minds and avoid facing those colleagues in front of whom we were insulted.

The girls are much more emotional on this aspect, and a small incidence hurts them more compared to teenage boys. Here, we have to be slightly thick-skin guys or girls, and we have to forget or ignore such incidences, or we have to take such insults as challenges for our life and always try to improve ourselves. Such insults happen during the class or in front of relatives when our teachers or parents insult us. The students keep that in their minds if they are publicly insulted because of a poor score or failure in an exam. It is the main reason for students going into depression and finally committing suicide.

Here we have to adopt a three-pronged strategy. First, teachers should not insult students publicly; they can call the students into their office and counsel them separately. Second, parents should refrain from insulting students in case of poor scores or failure in any exam, and they should not link the wastage of money to their wards' failures. Last but not least, the third point is that students should try to ignore such incidents, move on, and take insults or embarrassments as a challenge.

ix. Negative Thinking Versus Positive Thinking

There is a lot of role of positive thinking in deciding your future and career. It changes your mood for study and gives you positive energy that will motivate you for further study. Hence, finally, it increases your stamina for study. So, sleeping with positive thoughts will give you a comfortable, relaxed night's sleep, and in the morning, you will wake up again with positive thoughts and fresh energy.

But negative thinking induces a negative energy in the mind, and you will feel low. You will not be able to concentrate on your study; the sleep will be disturbed, and again, you will wake up with low energy and a tired body and mind that will finally disturb your study.

One thing you might have noticed in your life is that negative thinking comes automatically to your mind, but for positive thinking, you have to make some efforts. The flow of negative thoughts in our minds is an effortless activity and is a very normal behaviour of our minds. For positive thoughts, we have to make an effort in each and every second.

As an analogy, we can compare negative thinking to sailing a boat downstream in a river. Even if you don't sail the boat, it will keep moving, much like the flow of negative thoughts in our minds.

While the positive thought is like the sailing of a boat upstream in the river against the flow, unless you make the effort, the boat will not move ahead. Rather, it will move backward towards downstream, going towards negative thinking, if you stop sailing against the upstream.

A similar analogy we can have with games and study. In study, you have to make efforts, concentrate, and have a fresh, recharged mind. After a few hours, you will be enervated and tired. However, most games are effortless or only require physical fitness or an energised body; even if your mind may be cluttered with many things.

Hence, study, like positive thinking, requires efforts and playing games like negative thinking, is an effortless activity.

You can play anytime even though you are tired. Therefore, playing games can be used to recharge you for study, and study can make you feel exhausted, then you can play for a few minutes.

The negative thinking brings anxiety to your mind. Then, the anxiety results in depression, and the persistence of depression for a long duration finally results in a tendency for suicide. Hence, we have to stop this sequence at the initial stage of negative thinking only.

Positive thinking induces positive energy, encouragement, and motivation for your study. It reflects happiness and a glow on your face, which ultimately makes you fit and healthy. On the other hand, negative thinking can lead to irritation in your life. You may behave poorly towards others, make mistakes in exams or in life, or make wrong decisions for your future.

There are some antidotes for negative thinking. The first and foremost is to listen to motivational talks or speeches by a good motivational speaker, or read good anecdotes or stories. These may inspire you to study. Read interviews of great achievers, watch inspirational or motivational movies, or read good books on self-help or motivation. Do yoga or meditation for a few minutes so that your study will not be compromised. After that, you will feel energised with positive energy.

Another antidote for negative thinking is the "Fantasy." It was the technique we generally used during Civil Services exams preparation to ward off negative thoughts. A mild fantasy occasionally helps to remove negative thinking from our minds and fill us with positive energy.

Fantasy is an imagination of ambitions and their fulfilment in dreams. Just imagine you have achieved whatever you want.

If you are appearing in any entrance exam of Engineering or Medical, then just imagine you have become an Engineer or Doctor, after you have been admitted to a good Engineering or Medical College as per your aspirations. Similarly, if you are appearing in the Civil Services exam, then just imagine you have become an IAS or IPS officer. After such imagination, you will find that negative thoughts have vanished from your mind, and you are refreshed for studying.

Don't fantasise during the time which is most effective for study; instead, fantasise whenever you are exhausted and have free time after studying. Also, remember one thing: don't delve into fantasy too much. I used the word 'mild.' A fantasy of a few minutes is sufficient to energise you.

Remember one thing: fantasy is possible during the days of preparation for entrance of Engineering, Medical or for Civil Services examination; it becomes very difficult once you join the job. Fighting with negative thinking becomes tougher once you join the job because of family liabilities, office pressure, and real-life challenges. You have to come out of the cocoon of the protection of the parents, and you yourself will become the parents of some kids.

Last, for antidotes, are making a company of good friends and spending time with these friends who encourage you. Spend some time in religious places of your faith, or a few minutes listening to some soft, calm music, mainly instrumental, for good sleep or for positive thinking.

I hope that by adopting all these techniques, you can reduce the negative thinking from your mind. However, you cannot eliminate it completely; instead, positive thinking will eventually start prevailing in your mind for sure.

STAY POSITIVE, STAY BLESSED.

x. No Similar Things Simultaneously, Please.

Have you ever got confused in Charles' and Boyle's law for gases in Physics? The first is related to temperature, and the other to pressure when volume is considered for gases. Even today, many Indians may get confused between GATEWAY OF INDIA and INDIA GATE if they have not visited these in Mumbai and Delhi, respectively. Have you not used the words Angioplasty and Angiography interchangeably? Similar confusion arises with the bucket and basket in English. Whenever we open the glass door, on which it is written PULL or PUSH, then we think a little bit to compare these two words, and even then, we do the reverse in opening that door. It happens with me even today.

Here, I want to give one more tip to the students that will be very useful and will resolve their confusion in remembering similar types of things. Generally, we get confused in remembering similar or nearly non-distinct things even since our childhood. I want to quote a few examples where I personally found difficulties in differentiating the things and remembering them, generally mixing them up with each other.

In Physics, there was general confusion when studying Fleming's right-hand rule and left-hand rule, the difference between the functioning of a dynamo and a motor which are based on both of Fleming's rules, the working of concave and convex lenses and mirrors, the types of levers and their fulcrum, and the types of telescopes and their working.

In Chemistry, there is a litmus test for acids and bases that results in colour changes from blue to pink (or red), or vice versa. In English, there is confusion between 'its' and 'it's' and 'beside' and 'besides.' In history, the Battles of Buxar and Plassey, and among various Battles of Panipat create confusion in remembering. Similar confusion arises in Biology when we study the genus and species, various types of frogs, and the functioning of xylem and phloem. In maths too, whenever we study the integration of $\int \sec\theta$ and $\int \csc\theta$.

I am just quoting these examples to you so that you can understand that if two things are of similar nature, then don't try to read both simultaneously. Rather, read one thing and revise that 2 to 3 times then the other automatically you will understand and you will remember forever. Otherwise, you will mix up both and will be confused forever, and you may commit a mistake in the exam.

If you don't remember or study at different times, rather try to remember or study simultaneously, then much more time will be wasted on it.

Another easy trick to remember is that you have to make the diagram or notes at a different part of the page, and in a different colour. This way, your brain will take a picture distinctly of that, based on the placement and colour in your copy.

If you just remember Fleming's right-hand rule, dynamo functioning, or the xylem working, then you can easily recall the other opposite thing and its functioning quite easily.

xi. Stay Focused, Stay Targeted.

Have you ever thought that the movies we watched in the theatre, we could remember for decades, while the movies we watched recently on TV or OTT vanished from our memory in a few weeks? Or the movies we watched on TV in 1980, we still remember, but today we forget them in a few days if we watch them on TV.

Firstly, we compare the movies watching in the theatre with watching movies on TV at home. The movies we watch in the theatre are shown in one continuous slot, with only one intermission, and the entire hall is in complete darkness. Our focus is solely on the screen, and there is pin-drop silence from the audience. We are unaware of what the person next to us is doing. Therefore, our concentration and focus are entirely on the screen and its dialogue. We do not miss any dialogue because we cannot rewind the film as we do at home. At home, we can rewind or fast forward the film. Due to this concentration and focus, these theatre movies stay in our minds for decades. I still recall movies from 1984 that I watched at Panna in Kumkum Talkies. It has been 40 years, yet I vividly remember many scenes from various movies.

But when we watch the movies today at home in OTT or on TV, they vanish from our minds in a few weeks. The reasons are multiple.

Firstly, we watch the movie in the drawing room in full light, unlike in a theatre, while eating lunch or dinner. This way, our focus is not only on the TV but also on the other things happening nearby.

Secondly, the screen size is only 5% of the vision of our eyes compared to the whole room, while in theatre, it is nearly 100% because the rest of the hall remains dark, so we can see only the movie screen, nothing else.

Third, we have the option of using the remote to go backward or forward in the movie at home. Hence, this option makes us casual in listening to the dialogue as compared to in theatre, where we give a hundred percent concentration and attention so that we don't miss any scene or dialogue.

Fourth, there is only one break in the theatre in movies, but on OTT or TV, there are twenty-five commercial breaks in a movie of nearly 150 to 180 minutes. Hence, our mind diverts, and we start doing something else, if we don't have the option to fast forward the film. Here, our attention diverts due to these commercial breaks.

Fifth, we can start talking and discussing during the movie for any sensitive scene, by pausing the movie; again, it diverts our attention from the movie.

Sixth, in theatre, we watch the movie in a single spell, while at home, in the same movie of the duration of 150 to 180 minutes, we flip the movies or various channels and watch the movies in various slots or spells. Even my own family watches one movie over 3 to 4 days in various spells during only our lunch and dinner. Even in between one movie, we watch various other channels of news or songs, etc.

Now you can see that because of our hundred percent concentration and attention and staying focused on one film, we remember it for nearly 3 to 4 decades because our mind, eyes, and ears were engaged in one thing only, that is the film in the theatre. The same thing you have to do for your study also.

Now, we compare the film-watching in 1980 and in today's era, both on TV screens.

In today's film on OTT or TV, hardly could I remember even a few weeks of watching, but I remember the films of 1985 vividly. The reasons are, again, manifold.

Firstly, in 1980s we used to watch movies in a dark room by turning off all the lights, focusing solely on the 18-inch by 24-inch TV screen. We would watch the entire 150-minute movie in one go, with just one break and selected commercial ads. Nowadays, we watch movies in full light to prevent eye strain from the darkness.

Today, our focus is not entirely on the TV screen.

In 1980, there was only one channel of Doordarshan, so we did not have the option to flip channels. We were forced to watch only one programme at a time, and our memory was fully concentrated on that movie. There was only one movie telecast on Sunday evening (later changed to Saturday evening), so we could remember it for many years. Today, there are nearly 200 channels or more for movies alone, and we have multiple options. Therefore, it is very difficult to remember.

The purpose of these two comparisons is that we have to focus on selected subjects and only on selected books so that they will last in your memory forever.

Always remember the story of Mahabharata where Arjun could see only the eye of the fish to target. Nothing else he could see around because he was focused on his target only, and he was successful in that.

Today, there are hundreds of books by various authors. Hence, choose the best one and a few others for reference or clarification on any topic that is not clear from the best one. Reading multiple books at the same time will weaken your memory and grasping power. Therefore, first finish one book on any subject and only then move on to another book on that subject or any other subject.

Here I want to quote the name of one good movie of Jackie Chan that is "The Karate Kid." It is a very good movie on concentration, focus, target, and attention to only one thing, so that it will lead you to success.

During the class study, a student who is an all-rounder in Hindi, English, Humanities, Biology, Maths, Physics, etc., could perform poorly compared to the students who are experts either in Humanities or in Science subjects like Maths or Biology. This is because it is easy to be an all-rounder in junior classes, but as we progress to senior classes, we need to excel in only a few subjects, either Humanities or Science (Maths or Biology), to excel in any field. This is because the size of the books triples in senior classes, making it difficult to master all subjects with the same degree of expertise.

Similar is with the sports person; they have to concentrate only on one game instead of playing multiple games. Then, only they will be able to play in the Olympics. Hence, **STAY FOCUSED: STAY TARGETED.**

xii. Unique Tips From Friends and Mentors

We should never forget the friends, or any guide, or mentor who contributed to the success in our life. I want to quote the names of a few friends or seniors who guided me, and their guidance matters a lot for my career.

Puneet Modi guided me to purchase a book other than the normal textbook of the classroom. I bought a book, Children Knowledge Bank, for Rs. 20 in 1984 because of him. It was a very informative book for small children.

Vikas Chaturvedi and his father advised me to make photocopies of all the exam forms before submitting them or sending them by courier to the exam conducting authority.

Ajay Jadia, who was one year senior to me in my Engineering College, guided me to purchase "Word Power Made Easy" book by Norman Lewis. The book was very helpful in improving my English.

Mr Rajeev Jain suggested that I purchase the Collins Cobuild dictionary. He was a senior in my engineering college and the elder brother of my room partner, Sanjeev Jain.

Sandeep Rao, my batch mate during engineering, guided me that we have to seek guidance from the losers or unsuccessful participants as well as from successful candidates. Unsuccessful candidates will tell us the mistakes they have made, and successful candidates will advise us on the best approach. There is always a lesson in what to do and what not to do. Otherwise, we tend to seek guidance only from successful individuals.

Anil Jain, who was also my batch mate in Engineering College, was from the mechanical branch and belongs to Sagar (Madhya Pradesh). He guided me to read the questions of the chapter before reading the chapter so that there would be an interest in reading that chapter.

Pankaj Shrivastava, he was also my engineering batch mate. In Jia Sarai, New Delhi, we were preparing together for Civil Services. He was having mechanical as one of the optionals, and he was appearing in all exams of public sector undertakings. But my optionals were Maths and Physics, so I could appear only in Civil Services Examination or State Public Service examination. I told him about this limitation, then Pankaj guided me that because of only one exam, I devoted my whole efforts and energy only in one exam; hence, my probability will be more for selection because I am not diverted to multiple exams. Finally, he told me that multiple options make our determination weak.

Ashish Chandrawaskar, he was my engineering batch mate. He had a key ring made of wood on which was engraved with black font, "Keep Aim High." I was inspired by this three-word quote, so I always keep my aim high and never scared of tough targets.

Manish Malviya, he was also my engineering batch mate who was preparing for the Civil Service examination. I was inspired by his laborious skill. He was very lucky for me; it was his call in 1997 for the result of the Civil Services Mains examination that changed my life.

Mr. Hari Shankar Gupta (IES) was my Assistant Professor in Engineering College, who took classes for Basic Electronics. He advised me to choose Maths as an optional subject instead of Electrical for the Civil Service examination. This was due to the fixed schedule of CSE papers, with a longer gap between Physics and Maths papers compared to Physics and Electrical papers. Consequently, I decided against selecting Electrical as my optional subject and opted for Maths for the Civil Services Examination. This decision, made by me in 1992, proved to be very beneficial as Maths significantly boosted my scores in the CSE Mains.

Mr. Hari Ranjan Rao (IAS). He was also my college senior and the first IAS officer whom I met. He was a source of inspiration for me to appear in the Civil Services examination.

Mr. Ram ji Tripathi, he was with me since my 6th standard, although he was senior to me at Panna, but he guided me for my PET (Engineering entrance exam). He was with me until my final selection in the Civil Services examination. Ram ji is no longer in this world, but his memories are there in my mind forever. Due to my financial crunch, I borrowed all the books from him for the Engineering entrance exam and for the engineering degree, as our branch was the same, Electronics and Telecommunication.

Yogendra Bhadoriya, he was my school batchmate since 9th standard. He was always with me during my tough time and during my good time. I wish one day he would become a minister, or at least an MLA.

Mr Anand Prakash (IRAS) guided me in 2001 to do the LLB. He was my first boss in service at Bhusawal. I did my LLB degree from 2016 to 2019 at Bilaspur because of his guidance.

Paraag Jain (IAS 1996, Maharashtra cadre), guided me for Complex Numbers and Analysis, Integral Calculus, and Differential Calculus for the Mathematics paper during our stay in Jia Sarai. It is because of him that I scored well in Mathematics, especially in Complex Numbers, Integration, and Differentiation. Some of the books he suggested were very useful, and as a result, I scored 436 out of 600 in Mathematics.

Harish Ahuja, who was in Jia Sarai with me, told me about the solution that was launched in the market in 1996 for the Physics paper of the Civil Services examination. It was very useful in my 1997 UPSC exam.

Harish Ahuja always used to tell us that his mother said we should look at both palms and our lines daily, having faith in these lines of our destiny. These lines will never lead you astray unless you choose the wrong path yourself. It may take some time to yield desired results, but it will definitely happen. It's a matter of faith; just wait for the right time. Our duty is to work hard sincerely and honestly; these lines will never disappoint you.

Pankaj Saxena, who was one year senior in engineering from the mechanical branch, was with me at Jia Sarai, Delhi. I learned from him the sense of humour. He was an all-time happy and smiling guy. A little bit of an extrovert, I became because of him and his jolly nature.

Dr Mahesh Kumar Gupta (Khairha): He is my elder cousin brother practising as a doctor in the small town of Panna. He is always full of energy for serving others. His feelings to serve others (Seva Bhavna), sympathy for others are beyond comparison. During my absence, he was looking after both my parents (mother and father), and at the time of their illness, he was giving treatment and medicines.

These are just a few of the many people who have influenced my life. There are countless others—relatives, friends, and colleagues—who have left a mark on my life. I want to mention some more names: the late Mr. Vrindravan Khairha (my uncle), Sr. Christina, Dr. Arti Sharma, Ms. Bharti Sharma, Ms. Jyoti Chitranshi, Mr. Rahul Banerjee (scientist, son of my teacher Mr. Banerjee), Mr. Jayesh Chitranshi, Ms. Dimple Madaun (now Dimple Ahuja), Er.R.K Shrivastava (Principal Technical School Panna), Nitin Panigrahi (DASS), Mr. Naresh Salecha (IRAS, Member Technical, National Company Law Appellate Tribunal, New Delhi), Mr. Mohit Sinha(IRAS, Retired Member Finance & DG HR, Railway Board), Shri Amitava Mukherjee, Chairman-Cum-Managing Director NMDC, Mr. Ramji Meena (now Ramji Om, IRAS), Advocate (late) Mr. Vinod Kumar Verma, Jabalpur, Dr. Prashant Verma and all his sisters, Ms. Asha Lata Jain, Ms. Anjana Singh Bundela, Ms. Jaya Chaudhary (my engineering college's batchmate from the Computer branch), Ms. Manjari Gupta (her father was GM in NMDC Panna), Mr.Neti Prakash Chaturvedi, Rumni Ghosh, Mr. Kamal Kishor Sinha IRTS Divisional Railway Manager Dhanbad (my senior during engineering days), Dr.Priti Kimothi (my senior in my school at Panna) Ravish Sahay and Huzaifa Saifee (my hostel friend during engineering days). A special thanks to Samkalp IAS Organization, Delhi for the support and help in the Civil Services Interviews of 1996 and 1997.

I know the above names are not useful for the readers of this book, but you can take cognisance of these and learn similarly from your colleagues, seniors, or teachers. A small tip from them can change your whole life; any statement from them can become a motivational force for you, and finally, that can shape your future. Hence, always keep your mind, eyes, and ears open to take or accept new ideas and choose the best one suited for you.

xiii. Breaks Are Good for You

When you are deep in your studies, there will be some moments when the boredom will be overwhelming. And sometimes, despite your best efforts, you may face a test where your scores differ from what you hoped for. During such times, you might feel depressed and question yourself if all your hard work is even worth it.

In such a time, when you feel like you have hit rock bottom, do NOT keep pushing yourself harder. Instead, pause. Step away from the books and give yourself a break. Take a walk, watch a light-hearted TV show, or even go for a movie. Relax for a little while. This is not giving up; this is recharging.

Did you know Dmitri Mendeleev conceived the structure of the periodic table in his dream? He had a vision of the arrangement of elements, which helped him organize them based on their atomic masses and properties. This dream helped him create the periodic table we use today.

Another example is Charles Goodyear, who accidentally spilled rubber and sulphur on a hot stove. He noticed this process transformed rubber into a more durable material. Thus, this 'accidental' discovery of the vulcanization process revolutionized the rubber industry.

History has shown that many inventions happened either by accident or often during periods of inactivity, sometimes sleep. So, if history has shown us so many significant moments, relax, you are not alone. All you need is to take a break. And you never know that during such moments of relaxation, you may come across exceptional things.

When you take that break, you can also read something different, something out of the ordinary. It doesn't have to be directly related to what you are studying, but something interesting that still sparks your curiosity. It could be a random article, a biography of someone who inspires you, or even a fun science fact you never knew. It might seem irrelevant at the moment, but I promise you—these little diversions can lead to great discoveries later on.

When you are at home, you have the protection and support of your family. You can share your daily experiences with family members, feeling secure and supported. However, when you are sent to hostels far from home for exam preparation, you may feel lonely initially.

While some students adapt to hostel life, some struggle with homesickness, especially when their exam performance is poor. This loneliness is more common among emotionally and academically weaker students, who struggle to cope with the academic pressure and fall behind in their studies.

Top-performing students usually adjust better to hostel life because they find their studies interesting and can handle the pressure of supersonic speed of study during their classes. They gain new insights in coaching classes, which they might miss if they stayed at home. This positive academic experience helps them enjoy hostel life and look forward to a bright future.

If you are feeling lonely and stressed because something happened to you or some thoughts are disturbing you, all you need to do is communicate. You can communicate with your friends and parents about this. Discuss it with them and come to a proper conclusion. If you are still feeling lonely and homesick, as I said earlier, you can watch inspirational movies, listen to music, and listen to motivational talks on YouTube.

That's why I want you to remember this: when you feel most ineffective, depressed, or lonely, these are the right times when you might actually be learning something truly extraordinary. So, when you feel that weight of depression or frustration, don't let it overpower you; instead, turn it into a chance to learn something new to grow in unexpected ways.

Most of the inventions in history happened accidentally during the most ineffective or idle times of the scientists! Remember? During such moments, they weren't forcing themselves to focus on a problem. Just like them, when you allow yourself to explore something different during that depression or unproductive time, you may learn something exceptional, something you would never have come across during your regular studies.

Taking a break is important, but don't stay away from your studies for too long. The key is to find balance. Don't let the negative feelings overwhelm you in a way that they take over your mind or your focus for too long. It's about using your downtime to your advantage, not letting it consume you. So, take that break, explore the exceptional, and come back stronger than ever.

xiv. *Parents' Role in Empowering Students*

Parents play a crucial role in helping their children adjust to hostel life. It's important for parents to contact their children daily and visit them at least once a month until they settle in. Encouraging them to form study groups and socialize with other hostel students can help alleviate loneliness. Parents should also stay in touch with their children's friends to monitor any behavioural changes. If parents notice signs of severe depression, instead of scolding them or making them feel inferior, they should immediately visit their child and ensure they are supported until the situation improves. They should also have positive talks with their children, especially at this point in time.

Dear parents, when it comes to your son's or daughter's education, never think about how much money you have spent. No amount of money is more precious than their lives.

Another important point to consider is that instead of letting them stay in individual rented rooms, it's much better to have them stay in a hostel where they can live with at least a hundred other students.

Being in a hostel means they will be surrounded by friends and classmates all the time. This can make a big difference in their overall experience. They will have people to study with, share meals with, and talk to when they need support. They won't feel lonely or isolated, which can often happen when they stay alone in a rented room.

Living in a hostel can also teach them important life skills. They will learn to live with others, share responsibilities, and be part of a community. These experiences can help them grow into well-rounded individuals.

So, while it might seem tempting to give them a private space, the benefits of staying in a hostel far outweigh the convenience of a single room. Your child's safety, happiness, and personal growth are worth much more than the money you might save or spend.

If you see from the students' perspective, they must form a group of friends with similar academic goals is essential. Spending time together, studying, eating, and attending classes as a group can help prevent feelings of depression among children.

Additionally, students should engage in activities that uplift their spirits when they feel down. Listening to religious songs or bhajans, watching motivational movies like "Chak De" or "The Karate Kid," enjoying comedy shows like "The Kapil Sharma Show" or "Kaun Banega Crorepati," reading motivational books like "You Can Win" by Shiv Khera, or watching motivational speakers on YouTube can provide much-needed encouragement.

Daily communication with parents is vital. Students should share their experiences as if they were still living at home. Parents should also discuss a Plan B with their children in case they don't succeed in their exams, ensuring they understand that their worth is not solely determined by academic success.

Glossary

"It's fine to celebrate success, but it is more important to heed the lessons of failure."

– Bill Gates

AIIMS (All India Institute of Medical Sciences) Exam: This is the exam conducted by the Central Government of India for prestigious Medical Colleges called AIIMS in various States.

CAT (Common Admission Test): It is an entrance examination for PG courses in management for various IIMs of India. CAT is a computer-based examination conducted by IIM to shortlist candidates for the postgraduate programme.

CBSE (Central Board of Secondary Education): It is a governing body for students at the central level, which conducts exams and designs syllabus for all students who are studying under the Central Board.

Civil Services Examination (CSE): The CSE comprises two successive stages: the Civil Services (Preliminary) Examination (CSP) and the Civil Services (Main) Examination (Written and Interview). It is conducted by UPSC.

CLAT (Common Law Admission Test): It is the exam conducted for admission into National Law University (NLU) for law students. CLAT is a centralised, national-level government entrance test for admissions to twenty-two national law universities in India. Most self-financed and private law schools in India also use these scores for admissions to the law.

Collector or District Magistrate: They are the head of a district, controlling various departments in a district. They are selected through Civil Services examination or those who are selected in State Public Service Commission. They are promoted and made the district collector after promotion.

DANICS: DANICS stands for Delhi, Andaman & Nicobar, Lakshadweep, Daman and Diu and Dadra and Nagar Haveli (Civil) Services. DANICS officers are responsible for administering the civil administration of the Union Territory segments. They are group B officers who become SDMs (Sub Divisional Magistrates) in the union territories of India.

Doordarshan: Doordarshan is an autonomous Public Service broadcaster founded by the Government of India, which is one of two divisions of Prasar Bharati. It was the only TV channel in the 1980s in India.

GATE (Graduate Aptitude Test in Engineering): It is an exam conducted for entrance into PG courses in various engineering colleges and IITs. Recently, those candidates who are selected in GATE can also get the job in various PSUs (Public Sector Undertakings) of the government. GATE is an examination that focuses on testing a candidate's comprehensive understanding of undergraduate engineering and science subjects.

IAS: Indian Administrative Services. These officers are selected through the Civil Services exams conducted by UPSC. They are the heads of each district as Collectors or District

Magistrates. In the ministries, they head the department as Secretaries.

IES (Indian Engineering Services): These are class one officers who are selected through the Engineering Services Exam conducted by UPSC. The UPSC Engineering Services Exam (ESE), also known as UPSC IES (Indian Engineering Services), recruits officers to cater to the technical and engineering needs of the country.

IFS (Indian Forest Services): IFS is a part of the "Group A" Central Services under the Civil Services of India. The Indian Forest Service (IFS) is one of the most prestigious Civil Services in India, along with the Indian Administrative Service (IAS) and the Indian Police Service (IPS).

IIM (Indian Institute of Management): These are the prestigious management colleges in India located in various States. The CAT score or GMAT score is valid for admission to these colleges.

IIT (Indian Institute of Technology): These are the most prestigious colleges in India, located in various States, offering engineering degrees and M.Tech. Admission into IITs is based on the JEE Advanced score.

Indore: It is the biggest city of Madhya Pradesh, and it is also known as mini Bombay.

IOFS (Indian Ordnance Factory Service): The officers of IOFS are selected through the Engineering Services examination or Civil Services examination conducted by UPSC. The Indian Ordnance Factories Service (IOFS) is one of the Group 'A' services under the Ministry of Defence.

IPS: Indian Police Service. It is one of the three All India Services: IAS, IPS, and IFS. These officers are also selected through the Civil Services exams conducted by UPSC. They are the heads of the police department in each district as Superintendent of Police.

IRAS (Indian Railway Accounts Services): The IRAS is a Group 'A' Civil Service that one may get recruited into on clearing the UPSC Civil Services exam. Every year, the government appoints 25-30 officers. The IRAS officers are responsible for maintaining and managing the finances and accounts of the Indian Railways.

Jabalpur: It is one of the major cities of Madhya Pradesh and very famous for its marble rocks.

JEE (Joint Entrance Examination): It is an exam conducted by the Central Government of India for various IITs and NITs colleges. It is conducted in two phases; the first is JEE mains, and the second one is called JEE advanced. JEE mains is for all NITs and other engineering colleges, and JEE advanced is for admission into IITs.

Jia Sarai, Ber Sarai, Mukherjee Nagar, and Rajendra Nagar are the hubs of competition for various graduates for Civil Service examination and State PSC.

Jijaji: It is the husband of a sister, known as a brother-in-law in India.

JNU (Jawaharlal Nehru University): This is situated in Delhi. It is a very prestigious university with many schools that mainly offer postgraduate courses and research work in science and humanities, etc.

Kota: Kota is a hub of all coaching centres for Engineering and Medical entrance. Nearly four lakhs students study in the city. It is situated in Rajasthan state of India.

Motichur Laddu: It is an Indian sweet that is generally made during marriages and is considered a very auspicious sweet, offered during Indian marriages.

NCERT (National Council of Educational Research and Training): It is an organisation that is publishing various books for the students of the CBSE board or other boards. It is also conducting some talent search examinations. The NCERT is an autonomous organisation set up in 1961 by the Government of India to assist and advise the Central and State Governments on policies and programmes for qualitative improvement in school education.

NEET (National Eligibility cum Entrance Test): The NEET is conducted by the National Testing Agency (NTA). NEET is held for admission to MBBS and BDS courses in India. The test comprises three sections – Physics, Chemistry, and Biology.

NIT (National Institute of Technology): These are the prestigious Engineering Colleges of each state. Previously, these were called REC (Regional Engineering College). The score of JEE mains is taken for admission into NIT colleges in various States.

NLU (National Law University): They are organising law courses for the selected candidates under CLAT. These are the most prestigious institutes for a Law Degree.

NTSE (National Talent Search Examination): NTSE is a national-level exam conducted by the National Council of Educational Research and Training (NCERT) to grant scholarships to meritorious students studying in class 10th.

Panna: It is a small town and district place in the state of Madhya Pradesh, India, known as the Diamond City.

PET (Pre-Engineering Test): These exams were conducted in various States before the JEE for admission into state engineering colleges.

PMT (Pre-Medical Test): These exams were conducted by various States for admission into Medical Colleges of that state before the NEET exam.

Public Service Commission (PSC) of States: They are conducting exams for Deputy Collector, Deputy SP, and various jobs of government in various States.

SGSITS (Shri Govindram Sakseria Institute of Technology and Science, Indore) is one of the recognised engineering colleges in Madhya Pradesh.

Soan Papdi: It is a sweet that is distributed or gifted to various relatives or friends during Diwali, and is generally further circulated to other colleagues or relatives.

UPSC (Union Public Service Commission): It is a Central Government commission that conducts various exams for class one and class two officers, as well as other exams for defence. All the IAS, IPS, IFS, and other Allied Services officers are recruited by UPSC.

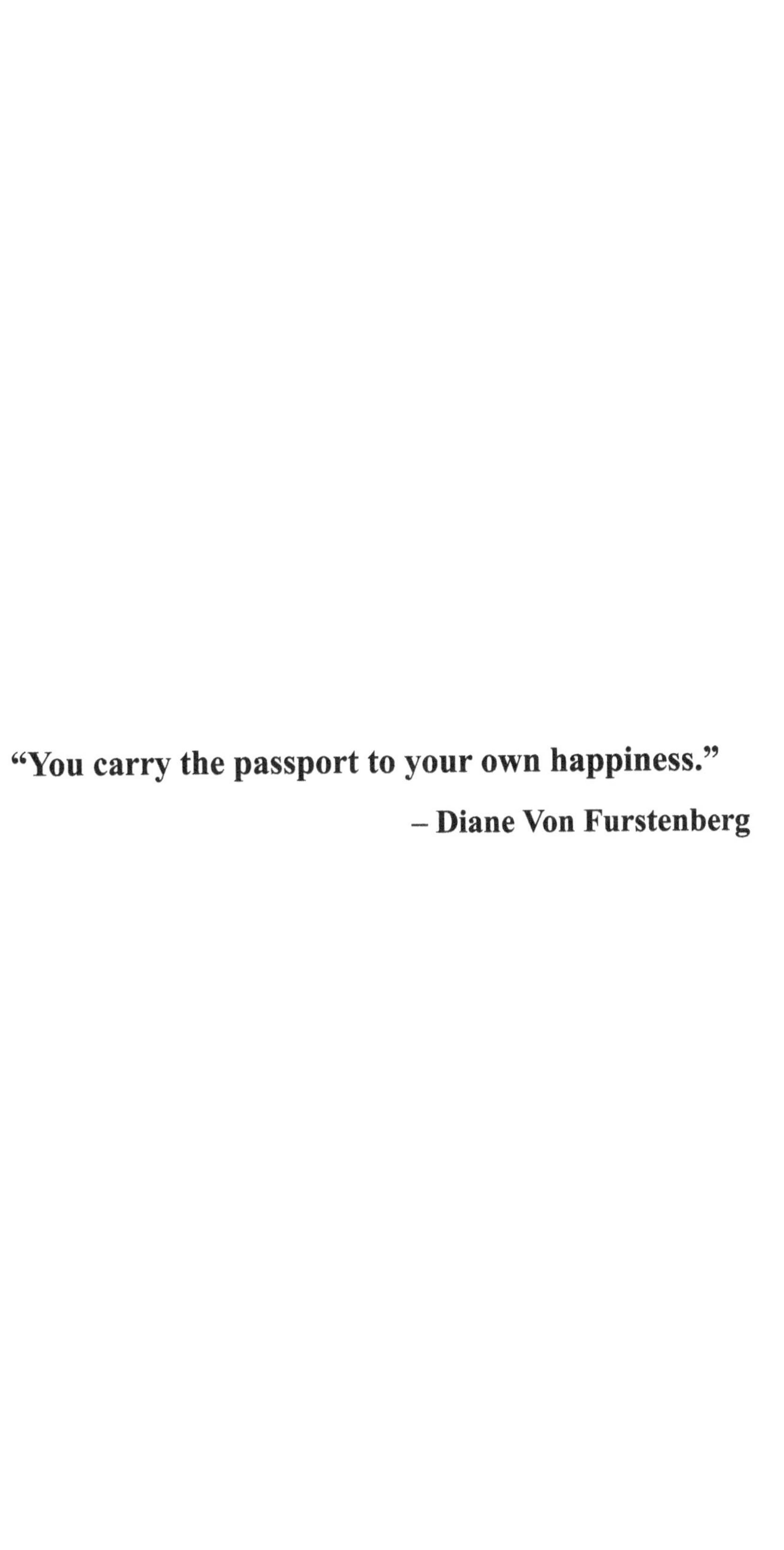

"You carry the passport to your own happiness."

– Diane Von Furstenberg

There is
no such thing
as
"final failure"

The author can be contacted for suggestions, improvements or feedback through his

 email: deepak.khairha@gmail.com

 Facebook ID: Deepak Kumar Khairha

 WhatsApp number: 9669883156.